When the Going Gets Tough, the Tough Start Laughing

When the Going Gets Tough,

the Tough Start Laughing

MARTHA BOLTON

MOODY PRESS

CHICAGO

© 1996 by
MARTHA BOLTON

All Scripture quotations, unless indicated, are taken from the *Holy Bible:
New International Version®*. NIV®. Copyright © 1973, 1978, 1984 by
International Bible Society. Used by permission of Zondervan Publishing
House. All rights reserved.

ISBN: 0-8024-9185-5

1 3 5 7 9 10 8 6 4 2
Printed in the United States of America

To friends who have laughed with us
and friends who have cried with us

To my family and special friends
Linda Aleahmad, Gladys Fox, and Rev. Gene Paul,
who walked close by through
some of the rough places in life

And to the many friends who have moaned
with us after one of my home-cooked meals!

CONTENTS

PREFACE

*T*he Bible tells us in Ecclesiastes 3:4 that there is a time to laugh and a time to weep. Most of us have done our share of both. Personally, I'd rather laugh. It leaves fewer wrinkles.

Both emotions are good for us, though. As much as we dislike them, tears and pain help us to grow. Laughter just makes the growing a little easier.

Life isn't a smooth, straight, level road. Most of us wish it were. It'd save us a fortune on Grecian Formula™, Excedrin™, and Rolaids™. But it's those ups and downs, those hairpin twists and turns, and those unforeseen detours that make life such an adventure. If we knew what was waiting for us around every bend, life could, and probably would, get awfully boring. We'd also get pretty confident.

Perhaps too confident. We'd rely on our own wisdom to face each new circumstance and wouldn't be dependent on a God who does, in fact, know precisely what lies ahead.

This book is about that journey through this life—with its trials and triumphs, testings and blessings, our blunders and His wonders. It's about those times when we couldn't stop laughing—and about those times when we thought we'd never laugh again.

And, as with any trip, whether we end up with memories of the flowers along the way—or the tumbleweeds that have blown across our path—will all depend on where we've been placing our focus.

1

IT'S A DOG'S LIFE, BUT LAUGH ANYWAY

I'm convinced some things happen to us for the sheer comedy of it all—you know, so life doesn't get boring. Like any good drama, life has to have a bit of comic relief to ease the tension and rejuvenate our spirits.

Take the time my husband did some work for one of our neighbors. He didn't expect any remuneration, but the man insisted on giving him a "little something" to show his appreciation. That little something turned out to be his full-grown, purebred pit bull. The dog came with papers, a month's supply of food, and incisors the size of the Washington Monument!

My husband tried his best to convince the man that a simple thank you was enough. After all, that pit bull was *his* dog, a part of *his* family.

We couldn't bring him into our backyard. His home was next door. We knew that, our neighbor knew that, and that tank with teeth knew that. But pit bulls have a reputation for being very territorial. As soon as he got used to our backyard, the owner explained, he'd be a wonderful watchdog, protecting our home as well as he had his own. All we had to do was give the animal time.

As it turned out, he didn't need much time. Within fifteen minutes he proved to be the perfect watchdog. The only problem was that he was protecting our home from *us!*

Our backyard became a mere extension of his, and we weren't even allowed back there! All day long Shredder (we took the liberty of renaming him) would pace back and forth by our sliding glass window, growling, snarling, double daring us to open it. To feed him, we had to wait until he was on the other side of the yard, open a window, toss out some meat, and close it again before his snapping jaws could get there.

This went on for about a week. We were prisoners in our own home. That dog owned the place. He wasn't making the payments to the mortgage company. He wasn't paying the utilities (although he did help bring down the electric bill by chewing through several wires). He wasn't helping us maintain the house in any way, but it was HIS house!

Our lawn chair became his throne, and our limbs were the chew toy of his dreams. All day long he'd stare at us through the windows, stalking our every move, waiting for the slightest slipup—a door left ajar, an unsecured window, an open screen. We could hear his breathing through the air-conditioning vents. We watched him growl at our shadows. Even the holes he dug made us nervous. They were rectangular and looked remarkably like burial plots.

In short, it wasn't working out. One of us had to find another place to live, and since he had less furniture to move, we decided it should be him.

Luckily, the telephone wires were still intact, so we called our neighbor and politely asked him to come over and repossess his dog.

We were tired of being pushed around by that four-legged battering ram with bad breath. We were fed up with paying for a backyard we weren't able to use. We had had enough of that canine bully leaving teeth marks in our stucco and trying to "fetch" the mailman. We were determined to give the dog back if we had to Federal Express™ him back!

Our neighbor was gracious, yet disappointed. He felt we were giving up prematurely. He thought we should give the dog more time to get used to us. After all, we still had most of our fingers left. Time would help us to emotionally connect. It would allow us to win over his loyalty. It would force us to bond.

But we didn't budge. The only bonding we wanted was with our backyard again—without having an ambulance on standby.

Eventually, the owner felt sorry enough for us that he let the dog return home. Until the day we moved, however, I don't think Shredder ever forgave us for continuing to live on "his" property. As far as he was concerned, we were trespassers, and it was his job to let everyone within city limits know it—twenty-four hours a day.

But that's all right. Thanks to all his barking, we didn't have to buy an alarm clock for years. He also taught us that it truly *is* better to give back than to receive.

2

BY
INVITATION ONLY

_S_ometimes the only thing keeping us from having a good time in life is ourselves.

Several years ago I was invited to a birthday party for a celebrity. It was a gala affair with hundreds of people in attendance, most of them movie stars. The red-carpet entrance was lined on both sides with eager paparazzi ready to capture their favorite celebs on film.

I wasn't a celebrity (my most important mail still comes addressed to "Occupant"), so I was certain I wasn't supposed to enter that way. Telling myself there must be another, less conspicuous, entrance for _ordinary_ folks, I embarked on a journey to find it. But all the other doors were locked, including the service entrance. There were only two ways to enter— down the red carpet with the other guests or behind the crowd of photographers, through the bushes, and under the red velvet ropes.

Wishing to remain as unobtrusive as possible, I chose the latter route. I hiked up my evening gown a few inches so it wouldn't drag in the dirt and began maneuvering through the bushes. It was a tight fit at times, but I knew the party would prove well worth my efforts.

When I reached the entrance, however, the photographers mistook me for someone trying to crash the party (I don't know why) and refused to let me through. I tried explaining that I indeed had an invitation, but when you're standing in the middle of a four-foot hedge with your high heels sunk in three inches of dirt, it's hard to look very convincing.

Frustrated, I walked around the building again, checking one last time for another entrance. I could hear the other guests inside, laughing and having a great time. That was where I was supposed to be—if I could only figure out a way to get in!

My husband, who had been patiently watching me all this time, trying his best to figure out what in the world I was doing, finally took me aside and said, "Sweetheart, you're making a scene. Your name's on the guest list. Why don't we just walk in like everyone else?"

Walk in like everyone else? What was he *thinking?* Had he lost all his social graces? We weren't anybody *important.* We were just us. We had driven up in a van, not a limo. He was in a rented tux with one sleeve shorter than the other. I couldn't even spell "paparazzi," much less walk through them. No, *my* way was the *right* way—unassuming, low key, and . . .

But wait a minute. My way wasn't getting us anywhere—certainly not into the party. Maybe he had a point after all. We may not have been as well known or as important or as rich as the other guests, but my name had been written down on that guest list in the very same ink as all the other names. (OK, so it might have been written in erasable ink, but it was there.) I had been personally invited by the host. I *belonged* at that party as much as anybody else.

Brushing a twig from my hair, I straightened my dress,

knocked the dust off my shoes, took my husband's arm and proceeded to walk down the red carpet, right behind Phyllis Diller. Cameras were flashing, and excited reporters were asking questions. Neither the questions nor the lenses were aimed at us, but no one was stopping us at the door and tossing us out either.

We walked on in, mingled with the other guests, and ended up having a terrific time.

I wonder how many times we do that in life—remain on the outside of the party, feeling sorry for ourselves as we peer through the window, watching everyone else having a good time, when all along we've been personally invited by the Host Himself to come on in and experience a lifetime of joy.

3

MAKING SENSE
OF IT ALL

*H*ave you noticed that some things in life don't make a lot of sense? But what they lack in logic, they make up for in confusion. For instance, does any of the following make sense to you?

—When you book a flight from LAX to Denver, why do they send you by way of Houston, then Orlando, up to New York, and back through Chicago before ever touching down in Denver?

—How come door-to-door salesmen can hear you in the shower and know you're home, they can hear you step on a twig in the backyard and know you're home, they can hear you roll over in your bed and know you're home, but they suddenly go stone-deaf whenever you say the word *no?*

—Why does it take longer to pump that last ten cents' worth of gas into your tank than it took to pump the whole fill-up?

—When grocery shopping, why are you mysteriously drawn to the one register that's ready to run out of tape?

—Why do you never think about whether or not you've turned off the oven until you're at least four hours into your vacation?

—Why is it as soon as you roll down the windows of your car to breathe some fresh air, you get stuck behind a bus and no longer have any?

—Why is it when you go out for a nice, quiet, romantic dinner with your sweetheart, invariably the hostess will seat you next to a birthday party for twelve four-year-olds?

—When you drive twenty miles out of your way to eat at a restaurant that serves your favorite dish, why is that the one dish they're out of?

—Why are napkin dispensers either empty or so over-stuffed that you have to pull out the napkins one fiber at a time?

—How come you never have car trouble when you've got plenty of time for it?

—Why do incorrect billing statements arrive only on Saturdays, making your aggravation fester until Monday when you can finally clear up the matter?

—Why is it when you run to the market in your grubbies, because you're only getting a few things and you're convinced no one you know will see you, everyone you know does?

—Why do car alarms accidentally go off only between the hours of 3:00 and 4:00 A.M.?

—Why do drivers who cut you off feel the need to honk at you after they do it?

—When you're in a hurry and only have time for fast food, why isn't it?

—How come when you have to make a flight connection, your departing gate will always be the one farthest away from your arrival gate?

—Why do companies think an automated telephone answering system that makes you go through the process of punching fourteen different numbers (getting disconnected twice) before ever being connected to a live person is a quicker way of doing business?

Throughout our day, we can't help but encounter many senseless frustrations. But what does make sense is maintaining our sense of humor about them.

4

FORBIDDEN
FOOD

*D*o you ever get the feeling that some health researchers delight in taking all the joy out of eating? It's as though they can't wait to add another one of our favorites to their ever growing list of forbidden foods.

They caution us against too much red meat, warn us about the high fat content of south-of-the-border cuisine, tell us to watch our potato chips and snack foods, and advise us on the negatives of too much salt, sugar, and caffeine. Adam and Eve didn't know how good they had it. They had only *one* kind of food they couldn't eat!

We're made to feel guilty if we don't skin our chicken, eat only egg whites, switch to imitation bacon, skim our milk, use artificial sweeteners, and replace cream pies and hot fudge sundaes with granola and rice cakes. And they wonder why there's so much more antisocial behavior than there used to be.

Choosing low-fat, cholesterol-free food items over those frosted, jelly-filled choices isn't an easy thing to do. But we can take comfort in knowing that we're not alone in the battle. If you don't believe me, just compare the health food section of your local supermarket to the Dolly Madison display. Which one has the dusty wrappers?

Frankly, I don't get worked up over the forbidden food issue, because what's harmful for us today may end up being good for us tomorrow. Remember the coffee controversy? First they said it was bad for us. Then they said it had certain benefits. Who knows where the debate stands today? And after years of being ridiculed and shunned, the poor egg is finally beginning to overcome its bad rap.

Which forbidden food item is going to be redeemed next? Real butter, fried chicken, country gravy, guacamole dip? It's anybody's guess.

I do know one thing. I'm going to be upset if, after years of my saying no to cheesecake, they suddenly announce that this high-fat dessert is actually a miracle food that somehow lowers the cholesterol level in our blood, builds up our immune system, increases hair growth in balding men, and takes away bad breath internally.

Growing up, we didn't worry this much about what we ate. I remember frequent dinners of only fried potatoes and gravy. Even those were cooked using leftover bacon grease from a jar on the stove. And once a week my mother would go to a local bakery outlet and buy so many glazed donuts and cupcakes that our kitchen looked like an outlet itself.

Then there was the chocolate gravy my father used to make every Saturday for breakfast. His own concoction, it resembled a warm, fluid pudding, and we would ladle it over a mountain of bread pieces. It was delicious, and I can't remember even once asking about its fat content. Today you'd be ostracized from your gym if you even mentioned such a diet!

But if we don't want dams forming in our veins, it's probably a good idea to watch what we eat—especially those of us who are regular churchgoers. There are all those after-church potlucks, fund-raising spaghetti dinners, ice cream socials, chili cook-offs, bake sales, Mother's Day banquets, Father's Day barbecues, Fourth of July picnics, Christmas parties . . . well, you get the idea.

The temptation to eat what we shouldn't eat, though, isn't anything new. As I said, even Adam and Eve faced it. And even though that forbidden fruit probably tasted delicious going down, don't forget they had to spend a lifetime working it off.

5

TWO
LINES

*T*here once was a man who had lived a very difficult life. He often compared himself to others and wondered why their life's journey seemed so easy while his was unbearably trying.

When he died and went to heaven, the first thing he saw as he passed through those pearly gates were two lines. Curious, he approached St. Peter and inquired about them.

St. Peter explained, "One line is for those who have endured great trials and tribulations while on earth. The other is for those who have endured little." Then, glancing down at his roster, St. Peter announced, "You, my brother, belong in the line on the right."

Satisfied, the man walked over and stood in his line. *At last,* he thought, *I'm going to be rewarded for all that I have suffered!*

After a few moments, though, he couldn't help but comment to the woman standing in front of him, "Does it bother you that while we were battling all our problems on earth, those people in that other line were sailing through life without a care in the world?"

The woman nodded in agreement. "No wonder they're all laughing and having a great time," she said. "If they had endured what I had to in life, they'd be too worn out to smile!"

"I know what you mean," the man replied. "I can't wait to see the size of *our* crowns!"

The clouds began to shift, and for the first time the man could read the sign above each line.

"Wait a minute," he said, a bit annoyed. "Our sign says this is the line for those who have endured little. Obviously, there's been some mistake."

He quickly excused himself, walked over, and stood in the other line. He couldn't answer for the lady, but he knew this was where *he* belonged.

The saints there welcomed him with open arms. There were even a few people he recognized from his life on earth— such as the old woman he used to pass on the street every day on his way to work. She'd always offered him a smile whether or not she got one in return. And usually she didn't. But that wasn't *his* fault. He'd had so many troubles on his mind. She'd understand that now.

And there was the coworker who'd made time to listen and offer words of encouragement whenever the man was feeling down.

And finally, there was the boy next door who had waved at him every morning and wished him a great day.

One by one they began sharing their personal stories. Never before had the man heard of such tragedies, such tests of faith, and such tales of triumph. Whatever problems he himself had faced paled by comparison. One thing was certain, he was in the wrong line.

Finally the boy asked the man to tell *his* story.

The man looked from face to face, recalling all the times these people had encouraged him in the midst of their own pain. He wondered why they hadn't told him of all the troubles they were facing. More important, he wondered why he had never asked. Without saying a word, he turned and walked away.

"Were there some people over there you knew?" St. Peter asked when he returned to the first line.

The man shook his head, then replied, "Some people I wish I'd taken the time to get to know."

6

THE JOY
GIVEAWAY

*S*ometimes the best way to keep joy in our lives is to make
sure we're spreading a little of it into someone else's.

I love stories of anonymous acts of kindness—thought-
ful gestures by total strangers, people doing good deeds to
others with no thought of reciprocation. Like the clown in
the Santa Cruz, California, area who dresses up and walks
the streets dropping coins into other people's soon-to-expire
parking meters.

Or the couple who used to watch a woman running after
her bus morning after morning, only to be left breathing the
exhaust as it rolled away without her. Instead of merely pity-
ing her, one day they decided to help her out.

They maneuvered their car in front of the bus and slowed
down, stalling just long enough for this poor woman to
board. To this day, the lady doesn't know it was because of
them that she got to ride the bus that day.

Another couple I know used to enjoy anonymously picking up other people's checks at restaurants. (I've tried to find

out which restaurants they frequent, but so far they've managed to elude me.)

Spreading joy doesn't always have to be done anonymously. After three Los Angeles police officers were killed in an early morning car accident several years ago, flowers, postcards, and other expressions of sympathy poured into the station. None, though, carried the impact of one particular gift.

A lone homeless woman, wearing worn-out shoes and a tattered coat, entered the station, clutching an imitation flower in a little plastic vase. She approached the officer at the front desk and, handing him the flower, explained that she had taken up a collection among her street friends. Together, they managed to raise enough change to buy the small flower in memory of the officers.

Sometimes all it takes is a hug. You have no idea how many people are walking around hug-deficient. Hugs don't cost anything (unless you happen to hug a pickpocket), and the benefits can be tremendous.

In the church I attended years ago there was a lady who gave hugs that would literally knock the breath out of you. One hug by her and for weeks you remembered you were loved (or at least until your ribs healed). I'm convinced Heimlich invented his maneuver after one of her hugs.

Smiles are free too (no matter what your orthodontist tells you).

So go ahead—spread a little joy around. And see how much of it ends up in your own life.

7

SUNDAY SCHOOL
LESSONS

When you think about it, the very first thing we learn to do in life is cry. The doctor spanks our bottom, we take in a breath—and cry. I'm not sure whether we're crying from the spank or from the quality of the air that's awaiting us, but we cry.

It's later that we laugh.

I married right out of high school. Everything went well at the wedding. I didn't knock anyone out when I threw the bouquet, and I hadn't made any of the food for the reception, so I knew my guests would be happy.

My husband, Russ, twenty-two at the time, had just joined the police force. We were excited about life, about marriage, about all that awaited us.

A few months after the wedding, I began feeling ill. I hadn't tried out any new recipes that week, so I ruled that out. When the nausea wouldn't go away, I scheduled an appointment with my doctor and soon had the diagnosis—I was pregnant.

We couldn't have been happier. We began making plans

to turn our extra bedroom into a nursery. We bought a couple of infant shirts (secretly hoping the baby would be a boy), and started counting down the days.

Unfortunately, our excitement was short-lived.

In my twelfth week of pregnancy, I began experiencing severe back pain. I went to bed, hoping that the discomfort was a normal part of pregnancy. It wasn't. By morning I had miscarried.

We brought the fetus to my doctor's office, and the diagnosis was verified. We had lost the baby. The doctor examined me, gave us some words of encouragement, then sent us home.

We tried to trust that God knew best, that all things work together for good for them that love the Lord. But what was so easy to quote in Sunday school class was much more difficult to put into practice in real life.

Still, we held onto the biblical truth that God is faithful. He has promised to go with us through the desert as well as to the mountaintop. He's there in our triumphs and in our disappointments. We knew this wasn't the end of this chapter of our lives. One day we would have a family.

The hurt would heal, and we'd laugh again.

8

THE WISE
IMPROVISE

One of the secrets, I believe, to maintaining a positive outlook on life is the ability to adapt well to circumstances, to improvise when things don't go as planned.

My father was great at improvising. One Christmas he made his own tree out of a broom handle and varying lengths of hedge branches. Decorated, it was surprisingly beautiful, and unless someone told you of its origin, you never would have guessed it wasn't a real Christmas tree.

There was hardly a car problem that Dad couldn't fix with a coat hanger and some electrical tape. From weak batteries to broken antennas, from loose exhaust pipes to missing door handles, Dad's home remedies always got the car back on the road again. (Or back in the ditch again if I was driving.)

And forget a home security system. Dad installed some of the most incredible and intricate traps all around our house to catch any would-be intruder. Traps that even Houdini couldn't get out of!

With his carpenter skills, he created beautiful pieces of

furniture out of nothing. Scrap pieces of lumber, old cans of paint, leftover nails would be turned into bookcases, shelves, and anything else his mind imagined.

The blueprints for incredible inventions and proposals for new, innovative industries were drawn on paper grocery bags or the backs of used envelopes.

He wouldn't let a shortage of supplies or a lack of formal training stand in his way. If he wanted to do something, he did it. If the conditions weren't perfect, he'd improvise. His mind was always active, thinking of unique ways to solve a problem rather than be defeated by it.

9

GO AHEAD—
RUIN MY DAY

*W*ouldn't it be great if we had control over bad news? I'm not talking about the kind we get from the media. I'm talking about the kind we get from people —people who can ruin our day simply by making one single announcement. An announcement such as:

"Thanks for letting me use your car this morning, Dad. By the way, do you have any touch-up paint?"

Or, "Mind if I sit here? I don't think this Ebola virus is all that contagious."

Sometimes the unnerving announcement comes right in the middle of your vacation:

"This is your pilot speaking. Please return to your seats. We have begun our final descent and should have you on the ground in about fifteen minutes. The plane should be arriving shortly thereafter."

Or, "I'm sorry, sir. It didn't go through. Perhaps you have *another* credit card we could try?"

Children are great at giving bad news reports. Hopefully, you won't ever get one of these:

"The new neighbors just pulled into their driveway, and I think they're rich! That's the third drum set they've unloaded."

Or, "Now, Mom and Dad, when my date gets here, try not to say anything about the tattoo on his arm . . . or the one on his neck . . . or the one on his face . . . or the one . . ."

Then there's this one: "I was outside playing ball this afternoon, Dad, and I think I've finally decided what I want for my birthday—a new window for the Petersons."

Unfortunately, we can't always control the bad news that comes into our lives. Sometimes we simply have to grin and bear it.

As I'm sure my husband will do when I tell him I've got good news and bad news. The good news is that I stayed under the speed limit the entire two-hour trip home from a recent speaking engagement. The bad news is it was because I had the emergency brake on.

10

BESIDE THE STILL WATERS

*S*omeone once said, "Experience is what you get when you don't get what you want."

Plans fall apart, people let us down, our hopes and expectations don't come to pass, life takes an unexpected turn. We get experience.

Less than a year after the miscarriage, my doctor confirmed what I already suspected. I was pregnant again.

This time the pregnancy went better than we could have hoped for. Friends and family gave me three baby showers. We painted and wallpapered the nursery in anticipation of the new arrival. We had made it. The baby was full-term now, active and healthy. The only thing left to do was wait for labor to begin.

Approximately one week away from my due date, my obstetrician failed to pick up the fetal heartbeat on the monitor. I tried to convince myself that nothing was wrong. The baby was simply positioned in such a way that we couldn't hear the heartbeat.

He sent me home, stating that if no heartbeat was detected at my next appointment, then labor would need to be induced.

All that night I asked God to let me feel something, the slightest movement, anything to let me know that the baby was going to be all right. All I felt was stillness.

The next morning, after several telephone calls between my medical doctor and my obstetrician, plans were finalized for labor to be induced that day. The medical doctor believed that if something had indeed happened to the baby, waiting another week could cause complications to my own health.

My husband drove me to the hospital, but it wasn't the same frantic drive we had rehearsed so many times. There was little excitement and even less conversation. We were both too busy praying.

Once admitted, I was taken to the maternity ward where a fetal monitor was attached to my stomach. Labor was induced, and for the rest of the day and into the night we listened to the silence of the monitor. The pain that silence brought was worse than the contractions.

In the early morning hours, after what seemed an eternity of hoping against hope, I delivered a 10-pound 2-ounce stillborn son.

For the next three days, I lay there in the maternity ward listening to the babies down the hall, turning away uninformed photographers who came to my room asking if I wanted pictures taken of my baby, answering telephone calls from concerned friends and family, and making burial plans.

We named the baby Hugh Leon after both grandfathers, and although we never got the chance to hold our son, we took comfort in knowing in whose arms he is resting now.

11

ONE AT
A TIME

*S*ocks come in pairs. They say deaths of famous people happen in sets of threes. We buy sodas by the six-pack. Life's irritations? They seem to come by the dozen!

I don't know why aggravations like to travel in clusters. They just do. If your washing machine stops working, your refrigerator will have sympathy electrical problems; your mechanic will report that your car needs a new transmission to go along with that new battery he's already installing; your daughter's teacher will call requesting a conference about her unsatisfactory homework assignment (the one you helped her with); your hairstylist will mix the wrong solution for your permanent, leaving you looking as if you bathed with the toaster; and you'll get a call from six different telephone solicitors all selling something you don't want, don't need, and can't afford.

Have you noticed, though, that our days are distributed singularly—only one at a time? No matter how much we try to rush them, how tightly we attempt to squeeze them together onto our calendars, they still come in twenty-four-hour increments.

Maybe that's the way we're supposed to live them.

When you think about it, no responsible newspaper would ever print tomorrow's news today. Or next week's. Or next year's. Tomorrow's news hasn't happened yet, so why would they waste ink speculating what it'll be? The few times they have jumped the gun and printed a story ahead of the fact, it was an embarrassment to all concerned. Just ask "President" Dewey.

Almost everyone was predicting that Dewey would be the next president of the United States. But Truman won a second term to the astonishment of the news media, the pollsters, and perhaps even himself. Bob Hope got in on the humor when he sent President Truman a one-word telegram. It simply said, "Unpack."

So even though our problems may not arrive alone, our days do. And when you think about it, living each day as it comes really does make sense. After all, who in her right mind wants to receive a year's worth of junk mail ahead of time?

YOU CAN TAKE THIS JOB AND *LOVE* IT

Well, he did it. George Burns made it to the century mark. Gracie would be proud of him. He vowed he'd make it to his 100th birthday, and he did.

Now the question on everyone's mind is, how'd he do it? What brand of vitamins did he take? Did he eat a high-fiber diet? Did he pass on saturated fats? Were his doctors the best that money could buy? Did he eat from the four food groups every day? Whose exercise video did he work out to?

According to George, his secret to a long life was simply this—"Love what you do, and get up and do it every day."

That's good advice.

I've been writing since I was nine years old, and I never tire of putting words on paper. It's my job now, and I love it. Over the years, though, I've worked at plenty of jobs I didn't care for at all. Like that one bozo job I had.

And I mean "Bozo" literally. My sister used to own a clown business. She would entertain at birthday parties, company picnics, grand openings, and any other special event. One weekend she discovered she had inadvertently booked two parties at the same time at two different locations. After much persuading, she coaxed me into taking one of them.

I wanted to help her out, but clowning just isn't my thing. The shoes are too small, and even though the white makeup gives me more color in my cheeks than I'm used to, clowning just isn't my favorite line of work. Still, I agreed to do the party. It was just this one party. What could it hurt? I thought.

I quickly found out that the best laid plans of clowns and men often go astray. Somehow I was given the wrong address. My clown sidekick and I drove around for an hour or so, totally lost. We stopped several times to ask directions, but no one took us seriously and refused to give us a straight answer.

By the time we finally arrived at the party, the kids were ready to use us as a piñata. We were clowns in big trouble, and believe me, a room full of people mad at a clown is not a pretty sight. We played some games, did a few tricks, and quickly said our good-byes.

Needless to say, I didn't volunteer for many clown jobs after that. But clowning around in my *writing* is something I've always enjoyed doing.

Only God knows exactly how much time each of us has been given. Why should we waste it doing something we don't enjoy? Too often people hate the job they're stuck in—and get up and do it every day. They're miserable. They know it, and everyone around them knows it.

George Burns had the right idea. Obviously many factors played into his longevity—his diet, his ability to handle stress, his genes, his general health. But he gave himself an additional edge by having a job he truly loved.

Not all of us can afford the luxury of pursuing our career of choice. But none of us can afford not to try.

13

BARKING UP THE WRONG TREE

From time to time we all have to put up with people who step out of line. If we're not careful, though, we might find ourselves judging their actions a little more harshly than they deserve.

The other morning while walking into our local post office, I was greeted with an irritating howling—one of those catcalls a woman sometimes gets when walking by designated hard hat areas. I thought, *Has society really come to this? Have we stooped so low that a girl can't even buy a stamp anymore without some Neanderthal ogling and making a scene?*

The howling continued, growing in intensity, all the way from my car to the post office doors. Finally I had all I could take. I usually would ignore such crude behavior, but this guy's wails were going right through me. He was acting like an animal, and someone needed to tell him so.

My speech was ready, my fuse lit, my righteous indignation couldn't have been more righteous. One more howl and this guy was going to get a piece of my mind if it was the last piece I had left!

Sure enough, the next howl came, even louder and more desperate than the others. The guy had to be stopped. I whipped around and glared in the direction of the sounds, but before I could open my mouth I discovered the caterwauling wasn't directed at me at all. In fact, it wasn't even coming from a man. It was coming from a rather large dog who was simply wailing about being locked up in a rather small car.

I couldn't help but laugh out loud at myself for getting worked up over a situation that existed only in my head. Embarrassed, I walked on into the post office, bought my stamp, and walked back to my car, with that dog howling the entire time.

I learned a good lesson that day. How easy it is to read more into a situation than is actually there. How many other times had I reacted to something that was merely in my imagination? Something I thought someone had said or did that had nothing whatsoever to do with reality?

In other words, I learned that judging a situation before all the facts are in will almost certainly land you in the doghouse.

14

LITERARY LICENSE

*I*n the months following the stillbirth, my husband and I tried our best to keep busy and regain some sense of joy.

That's when I decided to take a job as secretary at our church. A lot of important work and good counsel pass through the door of a church office. A lot of great comedy passes through it too. One particular incident I can recall had to do with a newsletter, a typewriter, and a secretary with far too much time on her hands.

This is how it went down:

One of the women, a quiet, wonderful, godly woman, had agreed to substitute teach our pastor's Sunday school class while he was away on vacation.

Disappointed with the turnout the first Sunday, she asked if I'd run a short appeal in the newsletter urging students to be faithful during the pastor's absence. I assured her I'd take care of it.

That next week when I typed the newsletter, I included a gentle nudge for Sunday school attendance, particularly in the pastor's class. However, I couldn't resist making a custom newsletter that only she would receive in the mail.

In *her* newsletter, that gentle nudging became . . . well, it became a bit more pointed. In the upper portion of the page I added a graphic of a woman jumping up and down in a huff. The caption, in half-inch letters, read, "GET OUT OF THAT BED, YOU BUNCH OF SLEEPYHEADS!"

The text went something like this: "The shepherd may be away on vacation, but that doesn't mean the sheep have the day off too! What do you think I'm here for? My health?!"

I filled the entire page with scolding, then closed with, "I'll be in class at 9:45 sharp this Sunday morning. You'd better be there too!"

I typed her name, made the back side of her newsletter look exactly like the regular one, then dropped it in the mail.

By midweek, I'd forgotten about it. That is, until one of the board members called to say he had received a distraught telephone call from a "certain sister in our church." She insisted that she hadn't said *any* of those things and that there was no way she could face the class the following Sunday morning unless someone went with her to explain the misunderstanding. She had only wanted a gentle appeal for attendance, not a reprimand!

"But, Martha," he continued, "I've read and reread the newsletter. I can't find any reason for her to be so concerned. Do you think she's been working too hard?"

Lucky for me, this wonderful woman of God also had a wonderful sense of humor, and when I finally explained to her—and the deacon—that she was the only one to receive that particular letter, we all had a good laugh.

Come to think of it, maybe that's why she has always encouraged me to put my humor into books. She must figure it's a lot safer there than in church newsletters!

15

FUNNY YOU SHOULD PRAY THAT

Did you know that some of our prayers can be funny? I'm not talking about that split-second grace we pray when we're starving (the one that could give our eyelids whiplash from how quickly we shut and open them). I'm referring to those prayers where we attempt to give God instructions on how best to run our lives.

Recently I was faced with a problem so complex that I had nowhere to turn but to the Lord. I should have turned to Him first, but that's how we are sometimes. It's like when we try to fix our own plumbing, then finally call in a professional plumber after geysers start erupting in the living room.

A few geysers were erupting in my life, so I figured it was time to quit trying to fix things myself and call on the Lord. I didn't totally hand over my problem, though. I figured I'd save God a little time by outlining all His options first.

"Lord," I prayed, "this is the answer I want." Then I proceeded to describe Plan A. I had reviewed the situation from every angle, and Plan A was clearly the perfect plan for me.

But it was only fair to give God a choice, so I also laid out Plan B, saying, "But this is the answer I can accept if I have to." Plan B did have a few drawbacks, but in the overall picture it was something I could live with.

Plan C? Well . . . I didn't like anything about Plan C. It was the one I didn't want, and I told Him that too.

Looking back, I can see it was a pretty hilarious prayer. It made as much sense as opting to stay awake during bypass surgery so you can give a few pointers to the doctor.

As the deadline for an answer to my problem drew closer, it seemed neither of my first two options was coming through. This, of course, called for desperate measures. I had already prayed. I had already presented my case. Now it was time to BEG!

"No, Lord," I pleaded. "Not Plan C! Please, please, pleeeeeeeeease, don't make me have to accept Plan C! I'll take anything else but not 'The Big C!'"

Begging was followed by the traditional Parade of Promises. We've all been the Grand Marshal of one of those, I'm sure.

"Lord, I'll double my offerings!"

"I won't miss a single church service, not even Missionary Sunday!"

"I'll . . . uh . . . I'll even . . . maybe . . . almost certainly consider, think about, perhaps quite possibly volunteer to teach children's church! Just don't give me Plan C!"

Do you think, when Moses got to the banks of the Red Sea, he outlined God's options or carved a stone tablet of promises to the Lord? Of course not.

He didn't pray, "OK, Lord, this is the way I see it. You've got three choices: Plan A is to show us some way to get around this water. Plan B is where You lead us to a pile of wood so we can build enough boats to get across. And then there's Plan C. That's the one where we just stay here and let the Egyptians capture us again. I don't think either one of us wants that, so let's forget I ever mentioned it."

Moses simply realized there was a problem and trusted God to work it out. And God did. God always has a Plan "D" (divine intervention) that's better than all the options we could ever dream up.

When I finally turned my problem over to the Lord—*really* turned it over to Him—He didn't come through with Plan A, B, or even C. He gave me His own Plan D, which I didn't even realize was available.

Like the parting of the Red Sea, it was a lot better than any of my plans, and there was absolutely no denying that it was God, and God alone, who had intervened. The answer He sent was one for which no one else could take any credit.

It's funny, isn't it, how often we try to limit a limitless God?

16

CLOSER THAN YOU THINK

*I*t wasn't easy walking by the nursery night after night, seeing the empty crib and silent toys, but my husband and I never gave up hope that someday God would bless us with a family.

We began applying at every adoption agency we could find. We had always talked about adopting children in addition to any we might have. We soon discovered that most of the adoption agencies had waiting lists longer than the Congressional Record. There was nothing for us to do but add our names and wait.

They say time heals all wounds, but being inundated with advertisements for everything from diaper services to baby insurance seemed to slow down the process. I packed away all the brochures and samples, believing that someday we would have use for them.

I filled my time now with writing and directing plays and comedy sketches for several congregations in our area. Russ busied himself with his work and leading a scouting program at our church. Even though we put forth a conscious effort to lay aside our disappointment and get on with life, the months passed slowly.

After several years of waiting and hoping, we decided to take a giant step of faith. We sold our memory-filled two-bedroom home and bought a four-bedroom house instead.

Our friends lovingly commented that we were nuts. We didn't have any children. Why would we need that big a house? And they were right. We didn't . . . now. But we were trusting that one day God would fill up those bedrooms. It was just a matter of time.

Unfortunately, we soon found out it was a matter of zip code too.

When I telephoned the adoption agencies to give them our new address, I was informed by several of them that since our move had taken us out of the county, we could no longer remain on their adoption list.

We were stunned. Our hopes were crashing and burning before our eyes. Were we going to have to start all over again? Had our giant step of faith turned into a giant step backward?

Our church was having special services all that week, but I didn't feel like going to any of them. I had already RSVPed to attend a major pity party. Mother's Day had just passed, and I was in no mood to listen to some evangelist tell me how much God loves me.

Instead of going to church, my husband and I decided to stay home and continue unpacking. We had been in our new home one week and were still in wall-to-wall boxes. Figuring it would be the easiest room to arrange, we decided to start in the nursery.

We hung baby clothes, moved furniture around, nailed up wall decorations. It seemed a bit futile to spend so much time arranging a room that wasn't being used by anyone, but we were driven to finish.

Russ was driven until about midnight. He had to go to

work early the next day, so I stayed up to finish the job, even though I was doing more crying than unpacking.

It wasn't fair. None of this was fair. We'd hear the news reporting stories of abandoned babies being found in trash bins, and here we had everything for a baby—and plenty of love—yet the crib remained empty.

After a few more hours of licking my wounds and being mad at God, I finally surrendered. I knew I couldn't go on harboring bitterness and resentment. God had already proved His love by giving His only Son to die on a cross. If He never did another thing for me, that was enough. Who was I to ask for more? I didn't understand why any of this was happening in our lives, but in spite of it all I vowed to continue serving Him.

I dried my tears, finished the room, and went to bed. That was around two o'clock in the morning.

At 6:00 A.M., the telephone rang. It was one of the out-of-state adoption agencies where we had applied, saying that they had a baby boy waiting for us, barely three weeks old! Four hours after I had given the matter over to God and ceased trying to work it all out myself, the answer came.

Needless to say, I was on the earliest flight I could get to the agency, too excited to even remember my fear of flying. Talk about an emotional high! The plane was cruising at an altitude of 30,000 feet. I was cruising at 35,000!

The agency worker met me at the airport and handed me the greatest belated Mother's Day gift I could imagine. We named him Russ, after my husband.

And Russ was just the beginning of God's blessings. Within the next two years, we adopted another son, Matt, at two days of age. Three and a half months after Matt came into our lives, I gave birth to our third son, Shane.

Our step of faith turned out to be a step forward after all. Our friends didn't think we were nuts anymore. In just two short years God had filled every bedroom.

17

BRACE YOURSELF

For the first few years of my life, I was bowlegged. *Really* bowlegged. I'd climb down from my rocking horse and look like I was still straddling it.

To correct the problem, the doctor prescribed braces, which I had to sleep in every night. It must have been difficult for my parents to make me wear those braces in spite of my very vocal protests (rumor has it my wails could break crystal). But they did it anyway because they knew what was best for me. I still have the braces, although I don't really remember wearing them.

I do, however, remember the cod-liver oil my mother made me take when I got a little older. She believed a daily dose of that foul-tasting stuff would help grow strong bones. She was right. My bones got incredibly strong from all the exercise I got running away from her each night!

Mom would eventually catch up with me and make me take my medicine, after which I'd gag and cry and pitch a royal fit. But thanks to her persistence, as well as my father's, I'm standing on a straight pair of legs today.

Some things we face in life hurt like those braces or are as difficult to swallow as that cod-liver oil. We don't see why we have to endure the pain and discomfort night after night. We'd rather run away and hide. We wonder why we can't just grow our own way, curved bones and all.

We need to realize that what is hurting us today may be the very thing that's going to strengthen us and help us to stand tomorrow.

18

PAST DUE LAUGHTER

*A*n image that will remain in my mind forever is of a lady I passed while visiting a friend in a psychiatric hospital. The woman appeared to be in her late fifties. She was sitting on the hallway floor, leaning against the wall, mumbling to herself. Her dark, unkempt hair and the worries of the world were both weighing heavily on her shoulders.

As I walked by, I could hear her one-woman debate. "I'll pay Sears this Friday and Penney's next week . . . No, I can't do that. I'll have to pay Sears next week and the electric bill this Friday . . . No, it's the water bill that's due this Friday. The phone bill has to be paid by next Wednesday . . . I know, I'll pay Sears and the phone bill this week, and . . ."

She was still doing her verbal accounting as I walked on to see my friend. This poor woman, I assume, had literally worried herself sick over paying bills. She had allowed financial woes to steal her joy and her mental health. I wanted to reach out to her. I wanted to offer some encouragement. I wanted to go home and cancel all my credit card accounts!

What I should have done was introduce her to one of the

deacons at a church I used to attend. This man, Frank Bush, took the pain out of paying bills, thanks to his remarkable talent for mimicking accents.

During the early years of our marriage, this dear friend would call our house the first of every month and pretend to be from a credit card company demanding to know where their payment was. Each month he'd pretend to be representing a different company.

Even if the bill wasn't due yet, he was so convincing I'd be talked into agreeing to mail the payment early to whatever address he'd give . . . usually his own or that of someone else in the church. I'd catch on eventually, and we'd have a good laugh over it. That is, except for one night when I was onto his shenanigans right away.

"So where do you want me to send the payment this time?" I asked sarcastically.

"The address on the envelope would be fine," the voice on the other end of the line said in accented English.

"The address on the envelope?" I laughed. "But that's so unimaginative."

"Where else would you like to send it, ma'am?" the voice questioned.

"How 'bout the moon?" I bargained.

My comment was met with dead silence, so I pressed on. "Do I make the check out to Elvis again? He still works there, doesn't he?"

"Ma'am, what exactly is your problem?" the voice asked, unamused.

"I'm not falling for it this time." I laughed. "You keep pulling this month after month, and I'm just not falling for it."

The voice grew a bit testy. "Are you going to send the check or not?"

"Are you going to send the check or not?" I mimicked.

"Well, are you?" he demanded.

"Hey, lighten up. I'm writing it out right now. That's E-l-v . . ."

"Look," the voice snapped, "if you refuse to mail your payment, I'm going to have to indicate this little incident on your credit report."

"My credit report!" I giggled. "Oh, that's good. You haven't used that one before. And by the way, you really do need to work on your accent. It's much too nasal."

The next sound I heard was that of a dial tone.

The following Sunday, I couldn't wait to confront that deacon.

"I'm really disappointed." I smiled knowingly.

"What are you talking about?" he asked, puzzled.

"You know," I coaxed, not buying his innocent act for one moment. "But this time, I'm happy to say, I was onto you from the start."

"I didn't call you this week," he said defensively.

"C'mon, don't try to get out of it. I know it was you."

He shook his head.

I searched his eyes for some assurance that he was joking. I found none.

"Then, that was a real call?"

He nodded.

. . . I wonder if there's still room on the hospital floor next to that lady. Now, let's see . . . I'll pay Visa this Friday, Sears next Wednesday, MasterCard on Monday, Penney's by the end of the month . . .

19

MULTIPLE
CHOICE TRIALS

Wouldn't it be great if we could pick and choose our trials? If we were handed a multiple-choice list on which we could circle all those tribulations we wouldn't mind enduring, while passing on all the "biggies"? Most of us would gladly take a bad hair day, a flat tire, a difficult person, or a traffic jam, over the death of a loved one, a debilitating illness, long-term unemployment, or a natural disaster.

There are plenty of good lessons to be learned from life's minor difficulties. Rush hour traffic teaches patience, flat tires develop coping skills, and a bad perm can give us a great lesson in humility. So do we really need to go through those more serious problems—the ones that keep us up at night, gray our hair prematurely, and cause us to bite our fingernails down to our elbows? Can't we let the prayer warriors handle those?

After all, what are a few mountains to someone whose faith can move mountains? Those of us whose faith couldn't budge a speed bump shouldn't have to take an "E" ticket ride through life. Right?

When Shane was born, we were so excited we hardly heard the doctor when he said the words "congenital heart defect." Further tests would need to be conducted to determine the extent of the problem and the necessary treatment. I couldn't understand why this turn of events had taken place in the midst of so much happiness, and once again all we could do was lean on the Lord.

After several days, the doctor discharged me from the hospital. Shane remained behind for further observation. For the second time I was leaving a maternity ward without a baby. But that was the way it had to be.

I called the hospital every few hours to see how Shane was doing. Friends and family continued to pray. By the time he came home, his condition had stabilized to the point that he was taken off his heart medication. The doctor explained that his heart defect would have to be monitored, and eventually treated, but for now Shane could go home.

With three babies in the house now, life got quite interesting. As soon as one would go off to sleep, another would wake up. Then when we got that one to sleep, the third one would wake up the other two. When one needed burping, they all needed burping. When one needed changing, it seemed they all needed changing. I remember praying for God to just help us to live until they were two years old. If we made it that far, we figured we could make it through the duration.

But all those sleepless nights, those crates of diapers (we'd buy them direct from a department store warehouse), and all those cans of formula lining our sink were a testimony to God's faithfulness. A testimony to God's faithfulness . . . times three.

20

POSITIVELY UNCERTAIN

On the journey from fear to faith, there can be a lot of funny.

For instance, do you ever feel God leading you to do something but just before you do it, you get cold feet? So you pray, "Lord, show me Your will."

Once you receive direction, you press on full speed ahead. That is, until your feet begin icing up again.

"Lord," you repeat, "I hate to keep bothering You, but could You show me just *one* more time that what I'm about to do is Your perfect will?"

He does, so you step out in faith. You're convinced that this is definitely His will for you . . . for sure . . . for certain . . . for the next five minutes.

Then the doubting returns.

"I don't mean to sound like a broken record, Lord," you apologize, "but could You show me just once more that I'm in Your will? I promise this'll be the last time I bring it up."

Again He gives you the assurance you need to move forward, but you soon discover that your feet haven't totally thawed out yet.

"OK, how 'bout if we make that three more confirmations," you pray. "That's all I'll need. Show me just three . . . no, four . . . no, five . . . make that *nine* more times, bringing the total number of reassurances to an even dozen. Then I'll know beyond a shadow of a doubt that what I'm about to do is absolutely Your will."

I wonder how many times God shakes His head and laughingly wonders, *What is it going to take for these people to learn to trust Me?* He brings us through problem after problem, crisis after crisis, testing after testing, and still we wonder if He's going to be there for us the *next* time.

God must have been shaking His head at me recently. He had been leading me in an area so foreign to me that I found myself stopping every so often for reassurance that I was truly walking where He wanted me to walk. I'd take a few steps, then stop, take a few more steps, then stop. (I realize my exercise program has that many starts and stops, but a walk of faith shouldn't.)

Then one night while I was reading my Bible, a particular verse spoke directly to my insecurities. "How long will you wait before you begin to take possession of the land that the Lord, the God of your fathers, has given you?" (Joshua 18:3).

I decided that night to quit going in circles concerning this issue and get on the path that God had chosen for me. We're always better off when we choose to take the journey He's mapped out for us. That doesn't mean there won't be some bumps in the road from time to time. But we can encounter those very same road conditions while walking in circles too.

The difference between the two paths, though, is that one will eventually get us to the Promised Land. The other will just get us dizzy.

21

THE FEAR CHANNEL

*L*ast week I watched a television special about sharks. It was interesting, educational, and it successfully convinced me never to set foot in the ocean again. It was followed by a documentary on meteor showers. That had me wearing a hard hat and shopping around for a steel umbrella for days.

Today I saw an advertisement on this same network for their upcoming *Hour of Tornadoes,* a travelog entitled "Camping Along the San Andreas Fault," and a three-night miniseries called "Snakes, Scorpions, and Spiders." Their "Killer Bee" update is still in production.

If you ask me, they should rename this The Fear Network. I cringe every time I watch it. Whether they're covering earthquakes, out-of-control comets, hurricanes, the dining habits of boa constrictors, or the world's most active volcanoes, they present their case well—there really *is* a lot to fear in this life.

I've squirmed my way through interviews with people who were bitten by a tiny brown recluse spider and lost their limbs and almost their lives. Survivors of shark attacks have given detailed accounts of the horror they endured between the jaws of a Great White. And those who miraculously made it through Hurricane Andrew or Hugo, or one of California's great earthquakes, all have had their stories to tell.

But too much of a bad thing can get you down. It can make you want to crawl into a dark hole—if you weren't afraid of black widows. Or go hide in the desert—if it weren't for all the rattlers.

When you think about it, though, there is far more to be thankful for than there is to fear. Consider all the hurricanes that never move onto shore, and the earthquakes that occur early in the morning instead of during rush hour, thus saving thousands of lives. Think of the countless storms that pass over us without forming a tornado, even though conditions are right for one.

And let's be honest, how many picnics have we had interrupted by a swarm of killer bees or incoming meteors? (The only thing I've ever had to put up with during a picnic is the ants, and they were just bringing back my home-cooked food from the last picnic!)

Granted, we should respect the weather, the heavenly bodies, and every creature God ever created, and we should use wisdom whenever we encounter dangerous situations. But when you get down to it, the Creator of the Universe is still at the controls.

Knowing that, is there really anything to fear?

22

SITTING ON "PINS" AND NEEDLES

*W*hen you think about all the different numbers we have to memorize throughout our lives, it's no wonder we're stressed.

It used to be we only had our Social Security, telephone, and driver's license numbers to deal with. Nowadays, everything has a number. We've got credit card numbers, answering machine access codes, and PIN numbers for everything from our checking account to our video rental cards.

I didn't realize just how many different numbers had been assigned to me until the other day when I called my credit card's 1-800 number to inquire about my available credit. From the moment that machine picked up the line, it was a downhill journey for both of us.

"Welcome to our convenient automated credit line. Please enter your account number."

I did that.

"For security purposes, and for your peace of mind, please enter your PIN number."

I did that too.

"Sorry, that is an incorrect PIN number. Please try again."

I reentered my PIN number.

"The PIN number you entered does not match this account. If you would like to speak with an operator, please stay on the line. If you'd like another chance to reenter your PIN number, you may do so at this time."

OK, so maybe I was entering the wrong PIN. I decided to try another number that I had in my head.

"Sorry, that is an incorrect PIN number."

Figuring I had inadvertently entered my savings account PIN number, I tried another four digits.

"The PIN number you entered does not match this account."

Well, maybe that was my telephone credit card PIN number. I tried again.

I was wrong again.

"If you would like to speak with an operator," the voice repeated, "please stay on the line. If you'd like another chance to enter your PIN number . . . and hopefully get it *right* this time . . . you may do so now."

I began entering every number I knew—my Instant Teller PIN number, my Social Security number, my driver's license number, my frequent flyer account numbers, my grocery store check cashing number, and, finally, my address added to my age, number of children in my family, and my grade point average in school, multiplied by my SAT score and divided by my systolic blood pressure (which happened to be steadily climbing at the moment).

"Sorry, but since you have failed to enter a correct PIN number," the voice said, "we cannot grant you access to this account. Thank you for calling."

"No, wait!" I pleaded. "I *know* my PIN number. I just need more time!"

I started pressing four-digit number combinations at random ... 7734 ... 9986 ... 3395 ... 2241 ...

"You have exceeded the number of tries you are allowed," the recorded voice insisted.

"C'mon," I cried, continuing to press numbers as fast as I could. "I know my code. Give me another chance! Maybe it's 6948 ... or 9375 ... or maybe 3390."

"Please accept our apology for any inconvenience this may cause you ..."

"4483. That's it! ... Or how 'bout 2951? 9964? 5128?"

"It's been a pleasure serving you ..."

"1148 ... 9963 ... 9024 ..."

"Do have a nice day," it continued, as I frantically pressed more numbers, "and please know that all of this is for your own peace of mind. Good-bye."

"And so is this," I said as the machine disconnected me. And I cut up the card.

23

OVERDRAWN AT THE MEMORY BANK

Guilt can keep us from a lot of things. It can keep us from enjoying that triple-scoop hot fudge sundae with the chocolate chip cookie sprinkles. It can keep us from hanging a hammock from our gym equipment when we know we should be working out. It can stop us from hitting that snooze alarm for the eighth time in a row when we should be waking up and getting off to work. It can also keep us from living in joy.

Life's too short to spend it singing those Could've, Should've, Would've Blues or The Regret Rap. Yesterday's gone. We can learn from it, grow from it, but we can't relive it. If we made a wrong choice here and there, then we know to make better choices next time. If we've missed an opportunity, we can be more prepared next time. But we've got to move on. It's a medical fact that people who spend all their days looking back will eventually get a pain in the neck.

They sometimes become one too.

Jesus said, "I have come that they might have *life*." He doesn't want us carrying the weight of every misfortune on our shoulders or wearing our faces so long we start tripping over our chins. He wants us to live in joy, not in the dumps.

Now, what I know about operating a computer is limited. I know how to capitalize all the wrong letters, how to inadvertently change fonts in the middle of a word, and how to underline everything on the page except the one word I want underlined. I know how to move a paragraph to where I don't want it, print sixty-eight copies of a page I only wanted two copies of, and type twenty-six lines of *r*'s because I left my finger on the *r* key too long.

But I do understand the "Delete" command. I've sent far too many manuscripts into computer never-never land by accidentally hitting that little key.

God's forgiveness is like hitting the "Delete" command on a computer. It gives us a fresh start, wipes the screen clean.

So the next time we feel our joy being stifled by regrets or memories of all those times we've failed Him or ourselves, we should stop and take another look at the computer screen of our life. We might be surprised to discover that our failures and shortcomings keep showing up because we're the ones working overtime recalling them from our memory banks.

Not God.

24

LAST MINUTES

During one of Shane's routine new-baby checkups, his pediatrician expressed concern that the soft spot on his head might be closing prematurely. He referred us to a neurologist who, after an extensive examination and X-rays, recommended surgery. The operation, he explained, would require an ear-to-ear incision and would take between five and seven hours.

We were concerned about such lengthy surgery, especially with Shane's heart condition. But after weighing the dangers of a premature closure, we agreed to go ahead with the operation.

The night before we were to take Shane to the hospital, I lay awake, alternating between worrying and praying. As a rule, the two don't go together, but every time I turned the situation over to the Lord, I found myself taking it back again.

It's funny, isn't it? We can trust God to hold the entire world in His hands, but we get nervous whenever we ask Him to hold our problems.

I don't know what time it was when I finally fell asleep. I do know it was late, because when the telephone rang the next morning, I could barely pry open my eyes. What the voice on the other end of the line had to say, however, woke me up in a hurry.

It was the neurosurgeon. He explained that because of Shane's heart condition, he felt it imperative to get a second opinion. He contacted the head of neurosurgery for our area, as well as the head of neurosurgery at a local children's hospital. After studying the X-rays, each determined that they had been misleading. The diagnosis had been incorrect, and the surgery was canceled.

I knew a little how Moses felt when he got all the way to the banks of the Red Sea before God parted it. Experiences like that are taxing on our nerves. But when you think about it, God parted the sea when Moses *needed* it parted. The surgery was canceled when it needed to be. It was at the last minute, but last minutes are His minutes too.

25

SORRY, I'M NOT IN RIGHT NOW

*I*understand the telephone company now offers a call screening service. All we have to do is give them the telephone numbers of any persons we don't wish to hear from, and calls being made from those numbers will not go through to our line. Simple as that.

What a great way to cut down on annoying telephone callers who challenge our joy.

As impressed as I am with this new telecommunications feature, the one I'm waiting for would be a bit more sophisticated. Mine would screen calls with regard to their subject matter. It would operate something like this:

Wrong number calls coming after 1:00 A.M. would be intercepted and saved until the same hour the following morning, at which time they would ring back to the caller's number, waking him up instead.

Callers who can talk for hours without ever taking a breath would be transferred to the time lady. Let them see what it's like to have to merely listen and listen and listen and never get a word in edgewise.

Insurance salesmen calling at supper time would be put on hold to a recording of Billy Joel's "Leave Me Alone." (I don't know why, but they always seem to call and try to sell my family life insurance right in the middle of one of my meatloaf dinners!)

Politicians who call seeking my vote would be advised to press "1" if they want to make a campaign promise or "2" if they want to retract a campaign promise.

Calls from college students requesting more spending money (but who haven't cracked a single book yet) would be transferred directly to Dial-A-Prayer.

Collect calls would be held until a credit check could be made to determine whether or not the caller's lack of funds is truly legitimate.

Calls informing me that I've won something fabulous, which cannot be mailed until I give them a major credit card number, would be automatically rerouted to the fraud department of the local police department for investigation.

Calls from self-absorbed people would immediately ring back to their own number so that they can spend the entire day talking to themselves about themselves.

And finally, calls coming just as I've climbed into the bathtub would be . . .

Never mind. There are far too many of those to even try to do anything about.

26

IT'S
ABOUT TIME

've never been very good at timing. The fire and smoke
damage in my kitchen attests to that. One Christmas my
kids bought me a sign for above my stove that reads
"Martha's Burn Center." Whenever I'm cooking a dish, I
usually have to rely on another family member or the fire
department to time it.

Trusting someone else's timing in the kitchen is much
easier than trusting someone else's timing in our lives. We
know ourselves, our schedules. Or so we think. We know precisely how long we can wait for that need to be met. We know
when we're overdue for that promotion. And we certainly
know that crisis we happen to be going through today would
have fit so much better into our schedule a month from now.

But our timing isn't God's timing.

Three heart catheterizations, an echocardiogram, and
numerous EKGs had determined that Shane would need two
separate heart surgeries. The optimum time for the first
surgery was shortly after his second birthday.

The Sunday before the scheduled operation, we asked the church to pray that everything would go well. This was new territory for us. We had handled scraped knees, stubbed toes, and sore gums from teething, but this was heart surgery. Once again, we were having to lean on God for strength.

When we admitted Shane into the hospital, however, preliminary tests revealed he had a slight fever, and the surgery was postponed. This routine went on for several weeks. The surgery would be scheduled, the surgery would be postponed. Scheduled. Postponed.

Frustrated, I had a talk with God about it. If Shane truly had to have the operation, then I wanted it over with. I wanted God to take care of him through it, but I longed to get on the other side of this crisis. Emotionally preparing ourselves for the operation (if that's possible), then having it rescheduled again and again was draining.

I know God heard my prayer, but apparently He decided not to do it my way. He can be funny that way. He looks out for our *best* interests instead of what we think we want. When once again we drove Shane to the hospital, it was determined that he had another low-grade fever, and surgery was once again postponed. I wondered why God was allowing this emotional roller-coaster ride to continue.

A few days later, as I was turning the television dial, a certain news item caught my attention. A reporter was standing in front of the medical center where Shane was to have his operation. He stated that a doctor there had just been diagnosed with hepatitis and the hospital was requesting that all patients who had been seen by a doctor in their pediatric ward within the past week return to the hospital for evaluation. Shane had only been seen by a nurse, then sent home, sparing him any possible exposure to the virus.

God knew what He was doing.

The operation was performed a week or so later, and

everything went well. Shane still faced one more surgery, but for now we could breathe a sigh of relief.

And whisper a prayer of thanksgiving, for God not only brought him through the operation, He also spared him from a danger we didn't even know existed.

God's timing may not be our timing, but it's always perfect.

27

A DIVINE
SENSE OF HUMOR

I'm often asked whether or not I believe God has a sense of humor. I'm convinced He must. Just take a look at a few of the unlikely people throughout history whom He selected for greatness.

Moses wasn't a great orator. He wasn't a member of Toastmasters and may even have had a worse mumbling problem than some of the order-takers at drive-through restaurants. Still, he was handpicked by God to be His spokesman before Pharaoh.

David, a mere boy with no military training and no high-tech weaponry, not even a lambskin flak jacket to wear, was the one God selected to defeat the giant Goliath and save the Israelites.

God could have chosen anyone to be the father of His people, but He gave the honor to 100-year-old Abraham. And to 90-year-old Sarah. Talk about a divine sense of humor! Sarah thought the idea was so funny, she laughed out loud when she heard God's plan.

God has even used animals. He caused a donkey to speak

to Balaam (and you thought Mr. Ed was an original Hollywood idea). And when Jonah was running from God and found himself tossed overboard by fellow seafarers, the Almighty sent along a big fish to swallow him whole and give him some time (and an atmospheric setting) to contemplate his disobedience.

Not only does God use the unlikely, but He often asks them to *do* the unlikely. He instructed Noah to build an ark in the middle of a desert, miles from the nearest surf shop. And as if that wasn't a funny enough scene, He had him start loading two of every kind of animal onto it. Now, let's face it, if your neighbor began doing something as strange as that, there'd be a For Sale sign on your lawn faster than you could say, "It sure looks like rain."

Joshua was a well-respected military leader, then God had him march his army around the city of Jericho seven times. Can you imagine what the people on the other side of those walls were saying? "This is the mighty warrior we feared? Is he wanting to do battle with us or hold a parade?"

But these unlikely men and women didn't let people's comments stop them from doing God's will. They went on to accomplish their seemingly unlikely tasks and became great examples of faith.

Moses went before Pharaoh and eventually convinced him to let God's people go.

Using only a slingshot, David hit a bull's-eye right in the middle of Goliath's forehead, dropping that mighty giant. Let's see Schwarzenegger pull that one off!

Abraham and Sarah had their baby from whom a mighty nation did grow. But their greatest testimony was that, at their age, they were able to survive the teen years!

The donkey's speech got Balaam back on the right track, and that three-day vacation inside the belly of a big fish convinced Jonah that trying to run from God is never a very good idea—even if he was surrounded by all the sushi he could eat.

When the people of Jericho saw their walls fall down flat, they stopped laughing about that silly army marching around their city.

And once the great flood came, Noah's friends didn't think the ark was such a ridiculous idea either.

Does God have a sense of humor? You decide. All I know is that when it comes to those who dare to do battle against Him, He always has the last laugh.

28

SUPER-GLUED

I remember a ceramic figure we kept on a shelf in our home when I was young that somehow survived five kids, numerous family pets, a few California temblors, countless blackouts, and more than its share of teen parties. Over the years, it had gotten knocked down, tripped over, broken in half, maimed, and accidentally decapitated.

Yet no matter what shape it was in, we always knew we could take the broken pieces to my father, and he'd have it back together in no time at all.

I'm not that skilled at making repairs. I tried fixing our toaster once. I managed to get it to work, but whenever the toast came up, the garage door would too. And whenever I repair a hem in one of my dresses, the staples start coming out after just one washing.

Ceramic figures, though, were my father's department. That's why we brought all cracked and broken figures to him. I don't know what kind of glue Dad used, but whenever he repaired something, it *stayed* together.

Sometimes life can leave us feeling like that ceramic figure. We endure a heartache here, face a disappointment there, someone may trip over one of our dreams or break our spirit in two. We might even fall flat on our face once or twice. When we're busy just trying to keep ourselves in one piece, we wonder how we can ever get back to a place where we can laugh again.

Maybe it's time to take all those broken pieces of our lives to Someone who has a proven record of fixing things. Maybe it's time to bring them to God. After all, when our Father repairs something, the bonding lasts.

29

PRIVATE GATHERING

I once knew a lady who spent her entire life deciding who *wasn't* going to be invited to her funeral. She made a list and gave her family strict instructions on how to discreetly plan her funeral outside the knowledge of this certain group of people. With each passing year, the list grew longer and longer. The relative who slighted her, the friend who betrayed her—all were added to the roll, and then some. It was the ultimate punishment, she figured.

It reminded me of that joke about the spinster who wanted only women pallbearers at her funeral. When asked why, she replied, "No man ever took me out while I was alive. They're certainly not going to do it after I'm gone!"

Just like that spinster, this woman carried her grudge to the end. And when she did die, her instructions were followed to the letter. Only approved family members and friends were notified.

On the day of the funeral, the deceased lay in her casket in the center of the chapel, all dressed up as if ready to welcome her *real* friends.

She would have been happy. Not one uninvited person tried crashing the service. Unfortunately, barely any of the invited mourners showed up either. Apparently, the woman had spent so much of her time sifting phony friends out of her life that most of her real ones fell through the holes too.

A few years ago I attended a funeral of a man who didn't want even God invited to his funeral. He had been hurt by some people at his church, and he, too, carried his bitterness all the way to the grave, requesting that no mention of God be made at his memorial service. It didn't matter that God wasn't the one who had wronged him. He was the one getting the blame.

Both of these people got what they wanted. Only God knows what it cost them eternally. It certainly cost them their joy while they were alive.

If someone hurts us, the Bible says we should forgive. But we shouldn't stop there. We need to get over the offense.

That's not to say our pain isn't real and justified, or that we should be a doormat and let another person continually walk all over us. It simply means that we should quit picking at all those old wounds and let them heal. We should stop dwelling on who's wronged us and concentrate on who we may have wronged. We should spend more of our time making new friends and less time crossing out old ones.

In other words, grudges should be buried long before we are.

30

MY
GOODNESS!

Are you a people pleaser? The type of person who can't say nnnnn . . . nnnnn . . . no? Do you spend so much time making sure others are happy, you've forgotten what it's like to have a good time yourself?

We could sure use your help with the annual charity garage sale. Can we count on you?

Absolutely!

Would you mind building a few game booths for our harvest festival?

Not at all.

The youth group is going to the show this Saturday—we might need you to chaperon. How 'bout it?

I don't know. My calendar's pretty full right now . . .

Please, please, pleeeeeeeeease.

Oh, all right.

We need one more driver for the Children's Church outing next week, someone to run the sound booth for the service this Sunday morning, and we could use some help on the church newsletter. What d'ya say?

Well ... I ... uh ...

Great! We'll be counting on you. By the way, how's your family?

My who?

Sound familiar?

Has it been so long since you've seen your family that they're thinking about putting you on the Missing Persons List? Do they have to hang your picture on your chair at the dinner table so they won't forget what you look like?

Do they need to call your receptionist for an interview with your screener to inquire about arranging a meeting with your booking agent to fill out a request for an audience with your manager, who might be able to set up an appointment with your secretary to discuss the possibility of a conference call with you?

And how about yourself? Are you so busy saying yes to that person and this person, this person and that person that you forget to budget any free time for yourself?

I'm all for volunteer work. It's one of the most fulfilling things we can do, and it can certainly bring a lot of joy into our lives. But if we're compulsively doing it at the expense of our families—and more important, if we're doing it in a futile attempt to be good enough to deserve God's love—we're fooling ourselves and wasting energy we don't have to waste.

It's like trying to pay a bill and having every credit card we own get rejected. We try our Discover card . . . *Sorry. Over our limit.* Visa . . . *Account expired.* American Express . . . *Overdue outstanding balance. Card rejected.*

Then Jesus comes along and puts down His Master's Card, and the transaction is completed.

In other words, our goodness can't earn what His goodness already paid for.

31

NO
SHORTAGE

*H*as this ever happened to you? A friend asks how your day is going, and the floodgates burst open.

"From the moment I woke up this morning," you whimper, "everything's gone wrong! First, I burned breakfast, which was no easy trick since I was serving cold cereal. Then a door-to-door salesman came by and took up two hours of my time. When I finally managed to get rid of him, I went out to my car to run some errands and discovered I had a flat tire. Can you believe that! Not one single thing has gone right today! I'd go back to bed, but one of the springs is sticking through the mattress, and you have no idea what it's doing to my back."

You could go on and on, but you've already taken up twenty minutes of her time, so in parting you try to be polite and ask, "So how's your day been going?"

Choking back her emotion, she answers, "My father passed away last night. And we just got the results back from my husband's cancer test—positive. My daughter ran away two days ago, and we haven't heard a thing from her . . ."

And you start looking around for a hole big enough to relocate into. You feel selfish to have gotten so worked up over trivial matters. By comparison, you've had a terrific day. You try to offer comfort, but now it sounds shallow and meaningless.

The more I talk to people, the more I realize that everyone has problems. Adversity isn't on the endangered species list. There's plenty of it to go around. And many times the one carrying the biggest burden is the one you'd least expect.

So if we're ever feeling overwhelmed with our own problems, we can take two aspirins and call the doctor in the morning. Or we can try listening to another person's problem for a while. Who knows? We may come to the conclusion that our troubles aren't so bad after all.

Or, to put it another way, walk a mile in someone else's pain, and we just might ask for our toothache back.

32

JOY IN
THE MORNING

Recently I was asked by a fellow comedy writer for the secret to writing humor when your own life seems to be unraveling around you. He had been finding it difficult to find laughter in the midst of pain, to see humor in life's hurts. It's not easy. But there is a sense of peaceful joy that comes in knowing that God has been there for us before, and He'll be there for us now—no matter what it is we're going through.

I'm convinced that's one reason trials come into our lives in the first place—to teach us to trust Him. Trust that He's in control and is leading us down the best path for our lives.

The night before Shane's second open-heart surgery was one of the longest in my life. I watched the clock as time slowly passed. Of the two operations, we were cautioned that this would be the more critical, involving putting Shane on a heart-lung machine while surgeons repaired a delicately located hole in the heart.

It was just Shane and I there in that hospital room—and God. Shane was sleeping. God wasn't. So I talked to Him.

I reminded Him of all the times before when He'd been there for me . . . as if He needed reminding. I told Him how much my children meant to me . . . as if He didn't already know. And I asked Him to go into that operating room and guide the surgeons' hands . . . as if He wasn't already planning on doing exactly that.

One thing I've learned through the years is that God is good. He loves us, and He loves our families even more than we do. And His love can be trusted.

The surgical staff came early the next morning to take Shane to the operating room. Family members gathered with us, as did our pastor, to wait and pray.

Several hours into surgery, word came, but it wasn't the news we wanted to hear. One of the doctors came out to the waiting room, and before he spoke a word, I could see something was wrong.

"At this point, we don't know," he said haltingly. "There have been a few problems. I wanted to prepare you . . ."

He returned to the operating room. I found an empty room there in the hospital and returned to my knees. None of this was making any sense. I didn't understand why I had miscarried the first pregnancy. I didn't understand why my second pregnancy ended in a stillbirth. And now I wanted someone to explain this turn of events. Why would God give us Shane only to take him back at barely two years of age?

Our church had begun a prayer chain, and those of us at the hospital continued to pray and wait. That was all we could do.

But it was enough. Not only did Shane make it through the surgery with no further complications, but he improved so rapidly that he was doing flips on the jungle gym in our backyard in less than a month!

Shane is now nineteen, and to look at his over-six-foot

frame, you'd never know he ever had two major heart surgeries.

When I reflect back on that day, I don't know how any of
us got through it. It's as though when we're in the middle of a
crisis, God gives us the exact amount of strength that we
need for the moment.

That's more than enough reason to smile.

33

IN YOUR
DREAMS

*M*any people don't have joy because of unfulfilled dreams. They haven't accomplished what they wanted to in life, so they think the only thing they can do about it is be miserable.

It's good to have dreams, goals, to know where we're headed. But if we don't win that Nobel Prize or become president of the United States, we shouldn't feel as though we've failed. Maybe our success will come in a different area. Maybe God has other plans for our lives.

When I was growing up, I thought I could sing. My brother and sisters and I would often be asked to sing at different churches. One of our favorite numbers was that old gospel favorite "In the Garden." It was the perfect song because the harmony of my siblings reminded the audience of birds singing in a garden—while I sounded more like the frog.

My delusions of talent didn't stop there. I also thought I could play the piano. Six years of lessons gave me that unfounded idea. My version of "No Tears in Heaven" brought forth plenty of tears here on earth. It's my own fault, though. I didn't really apply myself to my piano lessons. Every time my teacher would leave the room, I'd take ten minutes off the timer. The joke was on me, though. I found out later that every time *I'd* leave the room she'd take off ten minutes too.

Our son Matt, on the other hand, is extremely musical. He plays the drums (I've got hearing impairment to prove it), the electric guitar, the acoustic guitar, the bass, and the piano. He was blessed with an ear for music. I wasn't.

Even though I had taken lessons, even though my heart was in the right place, even though I longed to sing like Whitney Houston but sounded more like Sam Houston, God had a different plan for me. Those who have heard me sing say that leading me into writing instead of a gospel singing career is proof positive that God does love and protect His church.

So if God hasn't opened the door you want Him to open, and you're finding yourself trying to squeeze through a doggie door or crawl through the air-conditioning vent, perhaps you ought to stop and ask yourself—are you really doing what God wants you to do, or are you trying to force your own will onto your life?

The life God wants for us may be different from our dreams, but we can rest assured that it'll always be custom-made.

34

IMAGINE
THAT!

Most of the things I've worried about over the years haven't come to pass.

Growing up, I used to worry about my parents dying prematurely. They both lived to be in their seventies, saw their grandchildren born, and even a few great-grandchildren.

I've worried on airplanes too. (Just ask the stewardess who has to unclench my fingers from the armrest after landing.) But whenever I fly, the turbulence I *imagine* we're going to encounter is always worse than the turbulence we actually do encounter.

I've worried about surgeries that turned out better than I had hoped, dental treatments that were much less painful than I anticipated, and driving tests that I passed with flying colors. (Or was that flying instructors?)

In school I worried about oral reports. I pictured myself hyperventilating into unconsciousness right in front of my entire class. That never happened either. (I hyperventilated into disorientation and extreme incoherency but not into unconsciousness.)

I also worried about not passing foods class. (All right, maybe some worry is justified.)

Most of the time, though, worry isn't justified. My theory is that if God had intended for us to worry, fret, and live in anxiety, He would have made fingernails one of the four food groups. He didn't. So maybe we weren't really meant to dine on our acrylics. Maybe we're supposed to . . . trust Him.

A friend who was fighting a life-threatening disease knew about worry. She had every right to be concerned about her prognosis and wonder about her future. But she refused to be controlled by fear. She enacted what she called her Fifty Year Plan. Not wanting to look back fifty years after the diagnosis and realize she had wasted those precious fifty years worrying about not getting them, she decided to live each moment of life to the fullest. Her "winner" attitude is inspiring and contagious. She's been a cancer survivor now for more than a decade. I think her fifty year plan works.

So why let anxiety stand between you and a lifetime of joy? After all, worry is like bathing. It doesn't require any real courage, and if you spend too much time doing it, all you get are wrinkles.

35

GIVE ME
A BRAKE

*B*efore my father went to be with the Lord, he suffered a series of light heart attacks. During one of his many hospital stays, it became necessary to transport him to another facility for rehabilitation therapy.

The driver who was assigned to pick him up from the hospital arrived on schedule and carefully wheeled Dad up the ramp and into his medical van, making certain to secure the rear door.

What he forgot to secure was my father's wheelchair. Thus, at every stop sign, red light, crossing guard, and railroad track, this conscientious driver would come to a full and complete stop. My father, however, would not. His wheelchair would roll unobstructed all the way to the front of the van. Then, just as Dad would start to knock on the Plexiglas™ divider behind the front seat, the driver would press down the gas pedal, sending my father rolling back again.

This Bumper Wheelchair Ride continued throughout the entire trip. Unbeknown to the driver, my father would roll up, my father would roll back. Roll up. Roll back. For every mile that van traveled, my dad was traveling three. By the time they arrived at their destination, Dad was panting as though he had just run a 10-K in Phoenix in 110 degree heat! He was sweating, his hair was in his face, his clothing was askew, and he was hoarse from all the calling out he had done trying to get the driver's attention.

Needless to say, when the driver parked, walked to the back of the van, and opened the rear door, my father was ready for him. By not securing the wheelchair, this guy had messed up and messed up royally. This was supposed to have been a medical transport, not the Indy 500! An irresponsible act such as that could have cost him his job.

Some would say it *should* have cost him his job. But Dad merely looked the driver in the eye (when the world stopped spinning, that is) and laughed, saying, "That was better than a ride at Disneyland!"

My father had a great sense of humor. No matter how tense the situation, his dry wit could cut through it, encouraging everyone around him to take life a lot less seriously.

One thing I don't think I ever saw my father do was worry. That's not to say that he was in denial of life's problems. He simply chose not to make them his primary focus.

Dad knew he was dying. During hospital bedside chats, he'd often share his thoughts, his faith, his regrets, and his triumphs. But what I cherished most were those moments when he would freely share his sense of humor.

His prognosis wasn't something he had much control over, but he did have power over his attitude. His sense of humor was his armor against life's woes. And he wore it daily.

36

JOY
UNSHAKABLE

t's hard to hold onto your joy during an earthquake. It's hard to hold onto anything during an earthquake.

Natural disasters—hurricanes, tornadoes, earthquakes—seem to be occurring more and more frequently. But the Bible tells us that even in times like these, we should not be troubled.

I grew up in California, so I knew to expect a little seismic massage every once in a while. But two and three pointers were nothing compared to the early morning break dancing our house had been doing lately.

My husband and I were newlyweds at the time of the Sylmar quake. I've heard of marriages getting off to a bumpy start, but that was going a bit too far. Our block wall fell down in that early morning shaker. But even that was nothing compared to the more recent 6.8 Northridge quake. That morning, almost everyone in Southern California was awakened by a loud roar and violent shaking. I saw my entire life pass before me, credits and all.

My life had passed before me in other near death experiences (usually after one of my home-cooked meals), but this time it was as though it had lost its vertical hold. Everything was moving up and down—our bed, our house, our insides. Our solid oak chest of drawers, with each drawer filled to capacity, fell over like doll furniture. The china cabinet fell on top of our dining table, breaking most of its contents, including the goblets we used at our wedding. The mirror on our dresser snapped off, decapitating one of my childhood dolls, which had been knocked to the floor by the first jolt. My son's entertainment center fell over and hit the bed he had vacated seconds before.

With the power out, we had to walk through broken glass and climb over fallen books in the dark to get out of the house. Amazingly, no one got hurt. My family even claims the earthquake shook a few things *into* place at our house.

After that earthquake, material things took on a whole new meaning. In those thirty-five seconds we were reminded that none of the possessions of this world are of any *real* value. We can't take any of them with us. There won't be a carry-on baggage compartment on our flight to eternity, no pockets in our heavenly robes. The only thing we take with us is the record of how we've lived our life.

Now, when my husband and I go shopping, he'll point out the crystal vases and joke, "Honey, wouldn't these look lovely broken in half on our dining room table?" Or, "I wonder how this one would look in pieces on our living room floor?"

We still appreciate beautiful things. Who doesn't? But when you realize how quickly material possessions can be destroyed, it makes you want to concentrate on things eternal. It makes you want to do what Jesus said to do—lay up your treasures in a much safer place.

37

A LASTING
IMPRESSION

*H*ave you noticed that some of life's funniest moments
come when we're trying to impress someone and the
exact opposite happens? It's that total surrender to
embarrassment, that "I can't do anything about it so I might
as well laugh" attitude that can bring forth the heartiest and
healthiest laughter. It is healthy to laugh at our foibles, to take
ourselves and life's problems less seriously.

Recently I had the opportunity to do just that while
attending a convention of music professionals. A music video
that I had worked on was being honored, and I was invited by
the artist to attend his celebration and press conference. So I
did what I always do when I'm trying to make a good impression—I got dressed, changed, then changed again, and again,
and one more time before coming full circle and putting on
the outfit I was wearing in the first place.

Once dressed, I grabbed my purse and room key and
made my way down the hotel corridor toward the elevator.
On the way, I rehearsed my confident and professional
look—the one I use when I'm trying to impress industry big-

wigs or when I'm walking away from an instant teller machine that just chewed up my card and spit it back at me.

The look must have been working because I was getting more than my share of stares and double takes. It's interesting, isn't it, how we carry ourselves according to the reaction of others? The more stares I got, the taller I stood. The more whispers I heard as I walked by, the more determined my gait became. I felt in charge. I felt in control. I felt the strange sensation of something brushing against the back of my leg.

Figuring it was merely my imagination, I ignored it at first. But after the elevator ride, the walk down the hall, through the lobby, and past the front desk and gift shop, I thought I'd better turn and see what it was before leaving the hotel for the press conference.

When I looked back, I saw that it wasn't my imagination. It was my *nightgown*. Somehow it had gotten stuck in my belt, and I was dragging it along the floor behind me like a bridal train. (*Now* I know why the hotel desk clerk asked if I'd gotten enough rest the night before!)

Unhooking the gown from my belt, I quickly walked back to my room, dropped off the unwanted accessory, had a good laugh, and hid out until I was sure everyone who had been in the lobby was now gone.

By the time I arrived at the press conference, it was over. I had missed everything but the last few crumbs of refreshments. But at least I wasn't wearing any nightwear.

When you think about it, though, my new look could catch on and someday become the recommended attire for most business conventions. Then, when the speeches get so boring that attendees find themselves dozing off, at least they'll all be dressed for it.

38

A PERFECT EXAMPLE

I'm going to do so much for the Lord when I finally attain perfection. When I no longer have doubts or fears. When I quit failing Him and making mistakes in judgment, I'll be able to accomplish so much.

When I have all the answers to every question that will ever come up in life, think of the help I'll be to others. When I can honestly say I never feel discouraged or think that life's unfair, what an example of strength I'll be. When my house is spotless, my husband has no complaints, my kids never have a problem, and my dog stops turning up his nose at my leftovers, people will be eager for my wisdom (and my recipes). When I've successfully figured out how to divide my time so I can give 100 per cent to my family, 100 per cent to church work, 100 per cent to my job, and still have plenty of free time left for myself, everyone will want to know my secret.

When I've finally got my act together and I'm not missing a single cue, I'll at long last be perfect. After all, how can God use someone who's less than perfect?

The answer is, how can He not? Take a look around you. Imperfect people are all He has. The last perfect person to walk this earth was Jesus Christ.

We get confused. We think that as long as *we* have needs, we're not qualified to talk about God's providence. If we're faced with our own problems, how can we point others to His answers? If we hurt, how can we possibly speak of His joy?

The fact is, if everyone waited until he was perfect before attempting to do anything meaningful, nothing much would ever get done. The Scriptures tell us that some of the greatest men and women of God were remarkably flawed or felt inadequate for the job they were called to do.

Even David, the "man after God's own heart," was flawed. He committed adultery, then schemed to have the woman's husband killed in battle. Not exactly a model citizen. But God was still able to use a repentant David.

None of us is perfect. No one knows everything about everything. If we did, there'd only be one contestant on *Jeopardy*. We don't start out with all the answers, and, when we're taking that final breath, chances are we'll still be trying to figure some of it out.

But as far as I can tell, the only job requirement God looks for is a willingness to be the best we can be, to learn from our mistakes, grow from our trials, and follow His ways.

The perfection part is best left to Him.

39

NOTHING TO LAUGH ABOUT

At the close of church service one Sunday evening, a young woman made her way to the altar and requested prayer. She was in her late twenties, and her battle with terminal cancer was nearing its end. She had fought a brave fight, but now doctors had given her only a few more weeks to live.

Next to her stood another young woman. She was requesting prayer also, but for another reason—she had been contemplating suicide.

The contrast of these two young women was unsettling. One was weak and pale and hanging onto life with all the strength she had in her. The other was healthy and strong and wishing she could end hers. Life can be ironic at times.

When I was in my early teens, my best friend ended her life. We were only a month apart in age, and we grew up sharing everything—our clothes, our problems, our hopes, our dreams. And laughter. She had a great laugh, one of those you never forget—hearty and real. That laughter would sometimes get us into trouble when she'd sleep over and we'd keep my parents awake all night with our giggling. But it also had the power to make those day-to-day problems of teenage life seem to disappear.

This friend never knew it, but she was also a great encouragement to me with my writing. Back then I wrote a lot of poetry and would tape my poems on the wall above my bed (it was cheaper than wallpaper).

There were rows and rows of them—funny ones, serious ones, long and short ones, good ones, awful ones, poems that clearly expressed my feelings, and poems that no one could understand but me. Anyone who happened by my room would be accosted at pen point and forced to spend a half hour reading my wall. Needless to say, I didn't have a lot of visitors.

But this friend was different. Whenever she came over, she'd read my wall without any coaxing on my part. She'd eagerly look for new poems, reread the old ones, and laugh at all the right places. (Others laughed too, but it was usually while reading the serious ones.)

I've often wondered about this friend. What would her life have been like? Would she have pursued a career? Married? How many children would she have had? Would we have remained as close as we were then? Would she have been pleased that I did, in fact, become a writer?

The main thing I wonder about, though, is why on that night, at such a crucial moment in her young life, did she forget how to laugh.

40

OPPORTUNITY
TIMES THREE

Y ou can't back up the hands of time to recapture a missed opportunity. Sometimes, though, opportunity knocks twice. It might even ring the doorbell.

I realize this might be contrary to everything you've been taught, but recently I discovered that if you make the best of your missed opportunities, you could be surprised at what might come of them.

One evening a few years ago I attended a celebration for a well-known personality. Several former presidents were there, including Ronald Reagan. I had my camera with me and thought, *Wouldn't it be great to get a picture with Mr. Reagan?*

I handed the camera to my husband and, trying to be as discreet as possible, maneuvered my way next to the former president. Unfortunately, all the other people at the party had the same idea, and I kept getting knocked out of the shot. Finally I got up the nerve to simply ask if he'd mind having his picture taken with me. To my amazement, he graciously consented.

My husband positioned the camera, and the president and I posed for what was sure to be one of my most valued photographs. I couldn't believe my good fortune. I couldn't believe any of this was really happening. I couldn't believe . . . *the flash didn't go off!*

My big moment, the opportunity of a lifetime, was gone because of a dead battery. *(Where was that pink bunny when I needed him?)*

I thanked the president anyway and turned to walk away. As I did, I heard him say, "Would you like to try it again?"

Would I like to try it again?! A former president of the United States was giving my camera a reprieve and me a second chance. This was unbelievable!

"Do you mind?" I asked once more for reassurance.

He smiled. "Not at all."

We resumed our pose.

Unfortunately, the camera resumed its obstinacy.

Embarrassed, I thanked the president for his kindness, then disappeared into the crowd—disappointed, depressed, and determined to buy a new camera first thing in the morning!

I went ahead and had the picture developed and enlarged. There's nothing to see, but I framed it anyway and hung it up on my office wall. To everyone else, it looks like an 8" x 10" blank frame. *But I know it's me and the president!*

After I'd told that story at a banquet recently, a man walked up to me following the program and extended his hand.

He smiled. "So did you ever get that picture?"

"No." I laughed. "I had my two chances and blew it."

"Well," he said, handing me his card. "Maybe I could help you out. I'm pretty familiar with the man."

I looked down, read the card, then looked up again.

"Michael Reagan?"

He said he would see what he could do about getting me a picture.

A short time later, I received a telephone call from the former president's office. Mr. Reagan was inviting my family and me to have our picture taken with him. But this time, he'd use *his* camera.

So don't let a missed opportunity ruin your day. Laugh about it. And somewhere in the midst of your laughter, you just might hear it knocking again.

41

HERE COME THE LAUGHS

I recently read about a couple who had been married seventy-five years. When asked the secret to their wedded bliss, the man replied, "Neither one of us can hear anymore, so it makes no sense to argue."

In that single comment, that devoted husband revealed one of the true secrets to a long and happy relationship—a healthy sense of humor.

A sense of humor is important in any marriage. Think about it—you're seeing what each other looks like first thing in the morning. You've *got* to have a sense of humor!

Romance is a vital ingredient in maintaining a good marriage, as are common interests, commitment, and a God-centered home. But laughter can be a great pressure valve for those stressful times that just seem to come with life.

Laughter helps get you through those times when your wife accidentally runs your 100 per cent wool suit through the washer and now your daughter has the best dressed Ken doll in town. It can help ease the tension when your husband's barbecuing causes a four-block evacuation, or when your mother-in-law misspells your name on your Christmas card for the tenth year in a row. A healthy sense of humor also comes in handy when you discover that his last fishing trip pushed you over your credit limit, and now the corner gas station is holding you hostage for that $5 purchase that got rejected by Visa.

My husband and I have come to appreciate the value of humor. I'm not saying how many years we've been married, but the gift suggestion for our next anniversary is plutonium. And for the most part, we get along great.

Oh, he has a few pet peeves, which he enjoys bringing up now and then. For one thing, he doesn't like my eating in bed. But I tell him that salad bar doesn't take up *that* much room.

He also whines when unexpected company drops by during our private family dinners, even though I've told him time and time again that firemen, ambulance drivers, and emergency workers don't count.

My filing system tends to get on his nerves too. All he sees is piles of paper oozing from one room to the other without any sense of order.

But to the trained eye there *is* order. My order. My personal filing system took years to perfect, yet it's remarkably simple. Papers belonging in the D file are conveniently filed on the dresser, those beginning with the letter C can be found on the coffee table, the P files are inside the piano, and the S files are under the sofa.

Paying bills can also be a source of contention. We never seem to remember whose turn it is to mix up the monthly statements and whose turn it is to wear the blindfold and pick.

He resents the time I spend on the telephone, as well. He claims the receiver hasn't touched the cradle in over four years. This, of course, is a gross exaggeration. I distinctly recall hanging up briefly back in '94 during the Northridge earthquake. (All that shaking kept making me misdial anyway.)

Other than the above, we're remarkably compatible. We like the same kinds of food (anything I don't cook). We enjoy the same kinds of sports (whatever we can watch from our matching recliners). We also share our faith in God, a loving friendship with each other, and we both have tried to look at life with a sense of humor.

Every marriage will have its ups and downs, its good times and bad. You can count on it. But if you remember to put God first and keep laughter high on your priority list, you can make it through just about anything.

42

TRUTH IS
FUNNIER THAN FICTION

In my line of work, I've had the privilege of being around some of America's funniest comedians. Some of them are a laugh a minute; others save their comedy for the stage. Still, I can't tell you how many times I've seen a roomful of comedians and comedy writers go into a fit of laughter over something a stagehand, caterer, or chauffeur said, proving one very simple fact of life—comedy can come from almost anywhere.

A lot of great humor can be found in the newspaper (not just the Washington report, either).

Take for instance the headline I once read announcing the sudden death of a man who'd lived most of his seventy-plus years in the same county. In bold, one-inch letters the headline proclaimed, "LOCAL PIONEER IN GOOD HEALTH AT THE TIME OF HIS DEATH."

Several years ago I read another newspaper article about a local fast food restaurant. A customer had encountered a cockroach while dining there. The reporter asked the manager about the incident, and the manager was quoted as saying defensively, "I knew we had a mice problem, but I wasn't aware of any cockroach problem!"

Believe it or not, you can even get some great laughs in church. I don't think I'll ever forget the minister who was sweating so much during one of his spirited sermons that he finally asked, "Would someone open up a window and let some of this hot air out of here?"

Then there was the preacher who opened his sermon with, "I want to speak to those of you who perhaps are here this morning." And the one who wanted his congregation to be sure to greet all the visitors, so he asked the visitors to stand, then instructed the membership to "take a good look at these people and keep an eye on them after the service."

Children can be a great source of comedy. Like the young boy who simply refused to believe the truth about Santa Claus.

"He's really Mom and Dad," his older sister insisted.

"No, he's not!" the boy protested. "Mom and Dad can't buy toys for every kid in the world!"

One of my sons gave me a good laugh when he brought home a health form that he had filled out for his elementary school. Under "Blood Type" he had written, "Warm."

Another son wanted to know what his state name was so he could fill in the line on the form that said, "State Name."

Sometimes you only have to go as far as your mailbox to get a laugh. Just today I received an advertisement for a $49.95 book on how to pay off all my credit cards and get out of debt. The flyer also pointed out that they gladly accept Visa, MasterCard, Discover, and American Express.

Then there was the government report that referred to an airplane crash as "an excessive loss of altitude." And Oprah Winfrey's account of a time when she went into a bookstore to buy a book for a friend. She asked the clerk where she could find J. D. Salinger. The clerk replied, "He doesn't work here."

My favorite, though, happened at a press conference following the liver transplant of a famous personality. The doctor relayed to the press how seven organs from one donor had been successfully transplanted into six different people. A reporter inquired, "Is the donor alive?" After a stifled laugh, the doctor couldn't help but ask, "Are you a sports reporter, sir?"

Who knows where the next classic funny line will come from—Leno, Letterman, Bob Hope, your coworker, your eight-year-old, yourself? Wherever it comes from, one thing's for sure—life is the best situation comedy there is!

43

JOY FOR A LIFETIME

Some trials last a lifetime.

My eldest sister fought an ongoing battle with illness after illness from the time she was four years old. She died at forty-five years of age.

A bout with rheumatic fever as a child left my sister-in-law with three holes in her heart. Surgery was proposed, but back then her chances of a successful operation were only fifty-fifty. She opted not to take the risk and passed away on my fourteenth birthday, when she was only twenty-four years old.

As far as I can remember, neither of these two young women ever complained about her situation, looked around for someone to blame, or allowed herself to get caught up in self-pity. They knew they had a rougher road to walk than most of us, and they walked it with grace and courage, their love for the Lord never once wavering.

Night after night, my sister would sit at the family piano playing "There'll Be No Tears in Heaven." She didn't play forty-eight verses of "Nobody Knows the Trouble I've Seen"

—not on the piano and not with her life. She accepted whatever problems came her way, knew whom to lean on through them, and fervently believed that one day she'd be going to a better place.

One particularly vivid memory of my sister-in-law is of her singing that old gospel song "I Wouldn't Take Nothing for My Journey Now." It was one of her favorites. It was also her testimony. She passed away while serving the Lord on the evangelistic field.

How do you sing a song of triumph like that when you're facing the kind of life-or-death decision that my sister-in-law had to face? How do you keep your eyes fixed on heaven when you're in the midst of a lifetime of suffering, as did my sister? That kind of strength and inner joy can come from only one source. And His joy has a shelf life of forever.

44

THAT'S
THE BRAKES

As an experienced driver, I've noticed one thing—I can go a lot farther without my emergency brake on. It's funny how that works.

I don't always realize it's engaged, though. Oh, I know I'm traveling at only five miles per hour, and it's taking me three light changes to make it across the intersection. Then, there's that peculiar odor of burned rubber. But I don't see that my problem has anything whatsoever to do with me.

I blame it on a bad fuel pump, a battery that's getting ready to die, or my husband who didn't refill the tank after driving the car last. (The burned rubber smell I blame on the homemade cookies that I'm taking to the school bake sale.) I don't recognize the fact that the reason I'm not making any headway is that I'm trying to drive with my emergency brake on.

In life we can go a lot farther without our emergency brakes on too. Life emergency brakes come in all shapes and sizes. They can be fear of failure, bad habits, low self-esteem, or anything else that's holding us back from achieving our goals.

So the next time we start to grumble about not getting as far in life as we'd like, the next time we look around for whom we can blame for our shortcomings, maybe we should check our brakes. We just might discover that all along we've been the ones slowing ourselves down.

45

TILL DEATH
DO US CALL

Sometimes your situation is worse than even *you* realize.

Several months ago, I was planning a party to which many old friends were invited. As the RSVPs began coming in, I happened to mention to one caller that our former pastor had been invited and how much I hoped he would attend.

"You mean you haven't heard?" she gasped.

"Heard what?"

There was an uncomfortable silence, then . . .

"He died."

"What!" I said in disbelief. "I talked to him a couple of months ago. He was fine."

She went on to explain that she had heard the unfortunate news from several different sources. She couldn't recall how he died or exactly when, but our beloved pastor was no more. He had been whisked home in the prime of life.

I couldn't believe it. I couldn't believe he was dead, and I couldn't believe we hadn't heard a word about it. I owed much of my career to this pastor. Over the years I had "roasted" him mercilessly and played too many pranks on him to ever count. He was the pastor who had seen us through our son's two heart surgeries. We had shared tears, laughter, and friendship. There was no way that he would just pass away without *somebody* notifying us.

Determined to investigate the matter for myself, I hung up and quickly dialed his number. I'd extend my condolences, ask his widow if there was anything we could do to help, and apologize for not attending the funeral—which we would have attended had we only known about it.

After four or five rings, it was the answering machine that picked up the line. But it wasn't the recorded voice of a grieving widow. It was *his* voice. Robust, energetic, full of life.

Now I was *really* confused. Had he died and his family couldn't bear to erase his voice from the tape? Was he breathing his final breaths, but no one had the courage to let him in on the diagnosis? The sound of the beep was getting closer, but I couldn't think of a single message to leave.

How do you say, "Hey, you sound great, but didn't you just die?" Or, "We'd really like to get together soon, so shall we pencil you in for Friday or the hereafter?" Every greeting that came into my mind was either morbid or flippant. I figured the dial tone was the safest message to leave.

The next morning I got up the courage to call the number again. This time *he* answered. Live and in person.

"Hello . . ."

The voice made my heart skip a beat. He didn't sound like a dead person . . . not that I've ever talked to a dead person.

We talked and laughed and recalled old times. He sounded so carefree, I didn't have the heart to tell him about his death. I figured news like that could ruin his day. I was just thankful that we still had him with us.

It's funny how misinformation like that gets started, spreads, and virtually takes on a life of its own.

Some good did come out of this story. The reverend attended the party, and everyone who saw him there had the rarely afforded opportunity to say all those things they thought they'd never again get the chance to say to him.

After they regained consciousness, that is.

46

SURFING
THE CHANNELS

G roucho Marx once said, "I find television very educating. Every time somebody turns on the set, I go into the other room and read a book."

Yes, even television can sometimes tax our joy.

We channel-surf through the news that's following a high-speed police pursuit in progress, a docudrama about the rise of killer viruses, and a talk show on "Schizophrenics Who Don't Get Along with Themselves," and we wonder why we're not smiling.

Television does offer variety. There's a channel for almost everything—the shopping channel, the food network, court TV, all news, all sports, all classic movies. There's even a medical channel. (I hear they're wanting to add a waiting room channel that viewers will have to watch for at least an hour before they're allowed to turn to the medical channel and see a doctor.)

One of the major complaints about television is the violence. It used to be you only had to worry about seeing unnecessary acts of violence in television movies. Now they're in the news, on the talk shows, in the cartoons.

One thing that might help is the V-chip. The V-chip promises to give parents the option of blocking violent acts from coming through on their television sets. It's a great idea.

But why stop there? There are plenty of other chips that could provide a real service to the television viewer. Take, for instance, the C-chip. The C (or Calorie)-chip would block all those fattening food commercials from tormenting us at our weakest moments. Case after case can be cited of peaceful, law-abiding viewers watching these tempting and irresponsible ads and then committing violent acts on their refrigerators.

An OCL-chip would also come in handy. Otherwise known as the Over Credit Limit chip, this chip would automatically delete any shopping program once the viewer has hit his or her spending limit.

Fishing addicts would love a BW-chip. The Bad Weather chip would be designed to block out all foul weather forecasts from airing when their big weekend fishing trip is planned.

An R-chip would come in handy in election years. This chip, also called the Rhetoric chip, would censor from political ads all empty promises that the candidate has no intention of keeping. Imagine it—political campaign spots that speak only truth. Considering how many promises would have to be deleted, a chip like this could bring back silent films.

Sports widows would appreciate the S (or Sports)-chip. The way it would work is this: whenever the widow feels the sports addict has had enough, she simply engages the S-chip, and all football, baseball, hockey, basketball, golf, tennis, and frisbee competitions would cease from being aired, reviewed, or even referred to. Think what this would do for marriages across our country.

There are plenty of other chips that could greatly improve our lives. But for right now, I suppose the best television viewing chip still remains the one made out of potatoes.

47

TAKE TIME TO
COUNT THE COUPONS

My mother was an incredible woman. At seventy-two, she was well on her way to her third retirement. The building where she worked had changed ownership three times, and she worked for each company. When the building was sold, Mom went with it. It was as though she were named in escrow.

That's why it was so hard to believe when she was first diagnosed with lymphoma and given less than a month to live unless chemotherapy was started right away.

It had been only four years since my father's death, and a little more than a year since the untimely death of my eldest sister. It was devastating news.

My mother had hardly been sick a day in her life, so it took a while to convince her that she even had cancer or needed chemotherapy. But there wasn't any time to waste. Treatment was begun, and in the weeks that followed we saw a side of my mother that none of us will ever forget. She had incredible strength, unyielding hope, and a renewed appreciation for life.

My mother also knew that laughter was healing, both physically and emotionally, and tried to keep as much of it in her life as she could. Many times when the doctor would deliver less than encouraging news, Mom would wait until he had left the room, then, fighting back the tears, she'd urge, "Say something to make me laugh."

It wasn't always easy to find something to laugh about in the middle of a chemotherapy treatment, but somehow we'd manage.

With time off from work now, Mom's favorite activity became grocery shopping. Her routine was simple—wake up, get dressed, go to the doctor's office for her checkup or chemotherapy treatment, then it was on to the grocery cart races. Getting a shopping cart with all four wheels going in opposite directions didn't even seem to bother her.

We can learn a lot from people facing death. They remind us of what's really important in life—those things that we too often miss in our race from sunrise to sunrise. On our drives, she would notice the flowers while I was looking at the traffic jam. She'd see the children playing in the parks while I was focused on the potholes in the road. She heard the birds singing in the trees. I didn't even *see* the trees.

After months of steady improvement, Mom took a turn for the worse. She grew too weak to enjoy any outings, and it became depressingly clear that the end was near.

Knowing that Mom wanted to live more than anything else, the family opted to fight for her life with whatever means were available to us. I recall her joking with the paramedics who drove her to the hospital one night that all this "fuss" over her was ridiculous. She was fine. All she needed was some rest.

The next evening, the day before Mother's Day, she entered into eternal rest.

I have many memories of my mother—her hugs, her

laughter, the dozen or so pies she'd bring to every Thanksgiving or Christmas dinner (she felt each family member should have his own pie). I remember her self-sacrificing love, her gentle spiritual guidance, and her sense of fun.

Life wasn't always easy on my mother, but she knew how to make it fun. Through the good times and the bad times, her smile never dimmed.

48

BEEN THERE, FELT THAT

There's a store in our neighborhood that's open for business only during the fall months. It sells costumes, trick-or-treat bags, pumpkin decorations, makeup, everything you could possibly need for your harvest masquerade party.

Their biggest attraction is their masks. Whoever or whatever you want to be, there's a mask for you. Political figures, movie stars, cartoon characters, historical figures, monsters —they've got them all.

What the store's salespeople probably don't realize is that masks aren't seasonal. Some people prefer wearing them year-round. They help shield their vulnerability and keep others at a comfortable distance. It's too bad. Other than the Lone Ranger and a few other fictional heroes, people who wear masks aren't much help to anyone.

There have been many times when I've been encouraged by other Christians. But it hasn't been because of their mask of perfection. It's been when they've had the courage to drop all the pretenses and reveal their struggles—and how they made it through them.

I don't know why we get caught up in make-believing that we have no troubles. We pretend everything is fine, when we're right in the middle of a major crisis. It's as though we think we're not supposed to have problems, that we're less of a Christian if our journey isn't a smooth one. We put on a forced smile that fools all those around us, but who are we *helping?*

We were never promised a trouble-free life. In this world we're all going to face our share of disappointment and hurt. That person I sit next to in church might be going through a valley I journeyed through ten years ago. I might be able to encourage her. That bank teller you see every day may be going through the same trial you're facing right now. You might be able to encourage each other. We're all in this life together, and we need each other.

One of my first magazine articles was about my son's open-heart surgeries. I typed it up and mailed it off to a periodical that I had selected at random from a writers' market guide. A few weeks later the editor wrote back to say that not only did she enjoy my article, but her son was facing the same operation that following week. My letter and submission arrived just in time to give her the encouragement she desperately needed.

When we're hurting, we need someone who can say, "I've been there. I know what you're going through. I've felt that pain." Only when the masks come off do we truly help one another—and ourselves. Only when the masks come off can the *real* smiles come through.

49

AGELESS
JOY

*S*ome people lose their joy by aging. As the candles on their birthday cakes glow a little brighter, their outlook seems to grow a little dimmer. That's unfortunate. Losing our youth shouldn't mean we surrender our smiles too. But in the battle to stay young, too often the smiles are the first casualties.

As a society, we're constantly trying to stop the aging process. We think if only we could take off ten years, fifteen years, twenty years, we'd be happy. We're snipping and clipping, plucking and tucking, pulling and fooling. We liposuction the fullness from our hips and move it to our lips. We spend our day at beauty shops and tanning salons (I still say someone should merge the two and call it the "Dye and Fry"). We sing "Just As I Am," and some of us don't even remember what that was.

We try every means possible to stop time, but time marches on. I just wish it'd quit leaving its tracks across my face.

I'm not innocent in this wrinkle rebellion. I've done my

share of chasing the fountain of youth. Someone once told me that placing tea bags under my eyes would help get rid of that unflattering puffiness that seems to add years. I tried this, but all it did was turn my cheeks brown and give me an uncontrollable desire to talk with an English accent.

I've also fought those vision changes that come with growing older. I haven't bought glasses yet, but I don't know how much longer I can hold out. I can hardly read the instructions on medicine bottles anymore. I tried reading one the other day, and the only word I could make out was "WARNING!" I think the rest of it said something about not taking it on an empty stomach or in the same room as an elephant, but I'm not sure.

What I find most amusing about growing older is how our image of ourselves seems to freeze-frame at around seventeen years of age. My head thinks I can run and jump and do all the physical activities I did back then. My body, however, is clearly under a different impression.

It made its point recently when I accidentally locked myself out of the house. Hoping a back window had been left open, I climbed up on our six-foot block wall and prepared to jump. Growing up, I had done a stunt like this hundreds of times. I jumped off walls, trees, housetops, out of swings. All I had to do now was reenact one of those simple little jumps, right?

It took two-and-a-half days for my body to stop reverberating.

As soon as I hit the ground, I discovered that the spring I used to have in my step had rusted in place, and instead of my feet absorbing the shock, my teeth did.

But even if we're not as athletic as we once were, even if our biceps sag and our triceps drag, we should do whatever we can to see that our smile muscles never get out of shape.

50

ARE YOU TRYING TO TELL ME SOMETHING, LORD?

*H*ave you ever been in one of those moods? You know that you know that you know God loves you, but you'd just like for Him to somehow show you, somehow reassure you of that fact again.

Several years ago I prayed a prayer like that. I wanted to know that God really did care for me—even though He had already proved it time and time again. And time again. And time again.

In spite of my unfounded insecurities, I ended up being reassured of God's love that very week. But not in the way I expected.

Now, granted, all of the following could have been coincidence, but I believe the lesson I learned from it was no coincidence.

A few days after I prayed that prayer, the plumbing in our house went out to the tune of several thousand dollars, forcing us to move into a hotel for several days while it was being repaired.

That same week, one of our sons began having problems

with his vision, due to a head injury he had sustained in an accident. It became necessary to take him to a neurologist for further testing. That turned out fine, but on the way to the doctor's office, I got lost. Not the kind of lost where you merely pass your street. The kind where you can't seem to find the street anywhere on the face of the earth.

In short, everything that seemingly could go wrong that week went wrong. I thought, *This is how God is showing me that He loves me?*

Then I began to realize that God wasn't bringing any of this on me. But through it all I was learning a truth—how rarely I give thanks for all the things that go *right*.

Most of us are quick to pray when we have problems. But are we just as eager to talk with Him when things are going well? Do we thank Him for the many blessings He gives us every day?

God shouldn't hear from us only when we're in the middle of a crisis. He isn't FEMA. He's our Father. We should thank Him for the refrigerator that *didn't* go out, the car accident that *didn't* happen, the unemployment line we *didn't* have to stand in, the hurricane that's *not* forming off the coast by where we live, the daughter who *isn't* on drugs, the son who *didn't* get a ticket, the VCR that *is* working, the bills that *are* paid, the permanent that *did* take, the shopping cart that *is* operational.

No, wait. On second thought, that last one wouldn't be mere providence. That one would be a miracle!

51

LIFTING WEIGHTS

*O*ne of the things I remember most about my mother was her purse. Or should I say her "filing cabinet with straps"? She carried *everything* in there—bills to be paid, bills already paid, outdated advertisements, letters to be answered, answered letters to be mailed, church bulletins dating back two pastors, three years of canceled checks—and that was just in *one* of the pockets!

I wouldn't have been surprised if she was still carrying around the hospital receipt from my birth. Everything she could ever need, and plenty she would never need, was packed into that handbag.

In the months before her death, I was able to finally convince my mother to start leaving her purse at home and to carry only those few things she truly needed. It was difficult for her at first. She felt bare, empty-handed, even a little lost. But soon she realized how freeing it was, both physically and mentally, not to have to lift that kind of weight every day.

Some of us carry around just as much weight in our emotional purses. We've got a receipt for hurt feelings dated June 18, 1979; an IOU for one snide comment in response to one rude comment received on September 4, 1983; a raincheck for an encouraging word we had intended to deliver on December 6, 1992, but didn't; a voucher good for one defeated spirit (with our problems, we're *entitled* to it); and a coupon good for one negative attitude (no expiration date).

We carry all those old problems and hurt feelings around with us year after year, then wonder why we don't have the strength to smile.

Maybe it's time we start leaving our purses behind. Maybe it's time we set aside that emotional baggage that's been weighing us down and bring along only those things we truly need, such as forgiveness, love, inner peace, and joy.

They're a lot lighter to carry, anyway.

52

THEY KEEP GOING
AND GOING AND GOING

*O*ne of the best ways to retain joy is to stay active through every stage of life. My mother-in-law, in her late seventies, used to walk between ten and twenty miles every day, going from house to house, visiting families and inviting them to church. I heard of another grandmother who began a ministry to prison inmates in her senior years.

There's a man in our church who roller-skates with the youth group every chance he gets. He skates backwards, speed skates, does turns and figure eights and just about every other move you can imagine. He's in his seventies. His wife, close in age, designed and sewed more than fifty costumes for our Easter pageant one year.

I don't know why some people think that when they hit a certain age their talents are no longer needed. Nothing could be further from the truth.

Years ago I attended a church where the oldest member was probably in his early fifties. As lively as that church was, it lacked the inspiration and example that can come only from those who have walked with the Lord longer than most of us have walked on this earth.

We can learn so much from these wonderful seniors about steadfastness, about riding out the storms of life, about finishing the race. When a man in his eighties tells us that God has never once failed him, how can we not listen? When a woman in her nineties says if she had her life to live over again, she would have been stressed out over the bad times less and celebrated the good times more, that's good advice.

Sometimes we overlook these walking storehouses of wisdom and talent. We walk by them Sunday after Sunday and nod a greeting before moving on to our own pew. But we should pause and spend a little more time with them, find out what their talents are, and offer to put them to work. By doing that, we'd be adding a wealth of resources to our churches and helping to bring a little more joy into all our lives.

53

THAT'S A LAUGH

*F*red Allen once said, "It's bad to suppress laughter. It goes back down and spreads to your hips."

I don't know if he was right about the hips part, but suppressing something that's so good for us must be unhealthy. Laughter is good. It also puts those around us at ease (unless we're doing it while walking down the street alone). It eases tense moments too, like when your beautician accidentally mixes up your hair color with her daughter's Easter egg dye. Laughter is what gets us through our day, whatever it holds in store for us.

In fact, there are only a few times in life when the sound of laughter probably doesn't help the situation. For instance, you probably don't want to hear laughter when an IRS agent is looking over your return or when you've just asked your boss for a raise. Laughter is not the sound you long for when they announce your upcoming solo or when you ask your girlfriend's parents for her hand in marriage. Personally, I'd feel a little uneasy if I heard laughter after my waitress turned in my meatloaf order, nor is it what I want to hear from my bank teller when I hand him my savings account deposit slip.

Other than the above (and maybe a few more instances), laughter is usually a welcome sound. It reminds us that no matter what else is going on in our lives, for the moment at least, everything is OK. Perhaps Will Rogers summed it up best when he said, "We're only here for a spell. Get all the good laughs you can."

54

A MATTER
OF ATTITUDE

*T*hroughout our day things are going to go wrong. We don't intend for them to, but it's almost a given. Although we usually don't have control over these circumstances, there is something over which we do have control—our attitude. Keeping joy in our lives sometimes comes down to a matter of attitude. It's all in how we look at our situation.

When we're stuck in bumper-to-bumper traffic, we can rant and rave and scold our spouse for not listening to us in the first place and taking a different route, or we can look on it as an opportunity to read all those bumper stickers that usually fly past us at 90 miles per hour.

If we discover another family member has tossed his red sweater in with our load of whites, we can hire a private investigator to find the culprit, or we can start looking for accessories to wear with our brand-new pink wardrobe.

If our ATM runs out of money just as we step up to it, we can let that ruin our day, or we can be thankful the machine is forcing us into a mandatory savings plan.

When someone's tailgating us on the freeway, we can apply our brakes and give them a steering wheel sandwich, or we can wait patiently for that policeman who's three cars back and out of his view.

If we arrive at our favorite restaurant and are told there's a two-hour wait for a table, we can get irritated, impatient, maybe even start chewing on the potted plants, or we can find comfort in the fact that we're giving our body a two-hour reprieve before blowing our diet.

If we're the last one to take a shower and discover all the hot water is gone, we can kick the pipes, or pretend we're body surfing off Malibu in mid-December.

If we get a flat tire on our way to work, we can get frustrated, or we can think of all those calories we're going to burn off changing it.

After getting pulled over for a speeding ticket (which we clearly deserved), we can gripe and try to defend our actions, or we can be thankful that at least the incident isn't being videotaped for an episode of *Cops*.

Joy—sometimes it really is just a matter of attitude.

55

IF
ONLY

*H*ave you visited a collectibles store lately and discovered the current market value of that Mighty Mouse lunch pail, those metal Matchbox cars, that Oscar Mayer wiener whistle, and your original Barbie dolls which you threw out years ago? Remember that '57 Chevy you let go to the junk yard and all those old Elvis albums you gave away? How about that Shirley Temple mug or that Sheriff John badge? If only we'd known how much items like that were going to skyrocket in worth over the years, we never would have gotten rid of them. If only we had bought that vacant lot where the mall now stands, or that house that has since quadrupled in value . . .

But we can't spend our entire life in a world of "if only's."

"If only I had engaged the emergency brake after I parked on that hill . . ."

"If only I had believed all those signs that said, LAST GAS FOR 50 MILES . . ."

"If only I hadn't fallen asleep with that permanent solution in my hair . . ."

"If only I had remembered to save that 140-page manuscript on my computer before that blackout . . ."

"If only I had skipped that all-you-can-eat knockwurst festival . . ."

If only . . . If only . . . If only . . .

I remember waking up after the stillbirth and bombarding myself with a host of "if only"'s. If only the doctor had induced labor sooner. If only it had all been a bad dream. If only I could turn back the hands of time and rewrite this chapter of my life.

But the flatness of my stomach that morning told me it hadn't been a dream. It was very much a reality, and there was no turning back the clock. No matter how many "if only's" I pondered or how much I wanted the situation to be different, it was what it was.

We can't edit the events in our lives or erase those hurtful situations. What has happened has happened. We have to face it. We have to admit it. We have to go on. We need to turn our "if only's" into "in spite of's." In spite of our circumstances, in spite of our disappointments, in spite of having every reason not to smile, we still can.

56

PRICELESS JOY

According to the Bible, Gideon had seventy-one sons. But then, he didn't have to buy car insurance. The cost of living continues to climb with each passing day, and financial woes can certainly affect our joy.

Remember those good ol' days when a loaf of bread didn't take all our bread and our savings account balance had a number to the left of the decimal? Remember when a clerk would say, "Here's your change," and we wouldn't look at him as though he were speaking a foreign language?

When we first married, I'd spend $20 a week on groceries. Nowadays, I hit that by the second aisle (sometimes the first aisle if it includes the Hostess display). Express lanes are nice, but what we need is a second lane for customers with a full basket and a completed second trust deed loan application to pay the bill.

There was a time when gasoline cost 25¢ a gallon, and with a fill-up they'd clean your windshield. Now, it's around $1.50 a gallon, and the only thing that gets cleaned with a fill-up is your wallet.

Clothing has gotten expensive too. Especially swimwear. A bathing suit costs three times more than it used to for one-third the material.

The cost of housing has skyrocketed as well. Our first home cost $22,000. That'd still provide a roof over our heads today, but the walls would be extra.

If you listen to the economic forecasters, it doesn't seem that prices will be coming down anytime soon. So the only thing for us to do is grin and pay it.

The good news is that joy is free, and laughter is something we all can afford.

57

WHEN THE GOING
GETS TOUGH . . .

*I*n this life we're going to have troubles and blessings, failures and accomplishments, hurts and healings. Some things are going to go exactly the way we want them to go. Others may take a turn we didn't expect or want. We'll be let down by people we've loved—and loved by people we've let down. There will be times when we're on top of the world and times when we feel its full weight on our shoulders.

With everything that may come our way, we can still have joy. Not a joy that denies or discounts pain, but a joy that wells up inside of us *in spite of it.*

Laughter is a gift from God. It's not a skill we have to be taught. We don't have to attend laughter seminars or watch an infomercial on joy to have it a part of our lives. Laughter is a God-given tool to help us cope, to make our journey a little easier.

When I was little, my family would drive old Route 66 halfway across the country to visit my grandparents every summer. Along the way, we'd have flat tires, car trouble, we'd get lost, and that old-fashioned air conditioner my father would install in the car window would usually go out as we crossed the Arizona desert. But even with everything that went wrong, what I remember most is the laughter we shared.

The Bible says in Proverbs 15:15 that "the cheerful heart has a continual feast." It doesn't say only in the good times, when things are going our way, when our path is smooth and trouble free. It says a *continual* feast—in the good times, busy time, boring times, times of celebration, and times of crisis.

Knowing that, why shouldn't we permit our faces to give way to a smile a bit more often? Why not enjoy a hearty laugh every chance we get?

After all, when the going gets tough, the tough start laughing.